The Future is
small

Every owner of a physical copy of

The Future is Small

can download the eBook for free direct from us at Harriman House, in a DRM-free format that can be read on any eReader, tablet or smartphone.

Simply head to:

ebooks.harriman-house.com/futureissmall

to get your copy now.

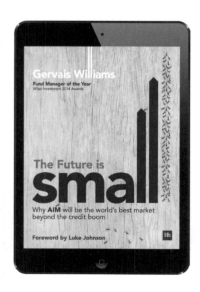

Gervais Williams

The Future is
small

Why **AIM** will be the world's best market
beyond the credit boom

Foreword by Luke Johnson

Hh

HARRIMAN HOUSE LTD
18 College Street
Petersfield
Hampshire
GU31 4AD
GREAT BRITAIN
Tel: +44 (0)1730 233870
Email: contact@harriman-house.com
Website: www.harriman-house.com

Paperback ISBN: 9780857194206
eBook ISBN: 9780857194213

British Library Cataloguing in Publication Data
A CIP catalogue record for this book can be obtained from the British Library.

Typeset by Harriman House.
Written with Mary Ziegler.
Internal layout and cover design by Stephen Taylor, Heat Design.

For my mum, Talitha Williams

The Alternative Investment Market (AIM) is an exchange that is all about the genuinely small. Rather like an anthill covered in pine needles, the AIM exchange is teeming with industrious activity that most overlook. In a world of challenge, ants symbolise the productivity and vibrancy of smallness; these key ingredients will deliver some of the best investment returns in the coming years and decades.

Foreword

Luke Johnson
Chairman Risk Capital Partners

This book makes a very straightforward proposition: AIM stocks should do well in the years ahead. I happen to agree with this theory, because it closely mirrors my own views and philosophy on investing, which have been arrived at during 30-odd years in business. As a consequence, I heartily recommend this volume to any reader who is willing to decide for themselves how to deploy their savings.

Gervais Williams knows his material. He has been a highly successful professional investor for over a quarter of a century. Unlike many authors of similar books, he is an active participant in the market, not simply an academic whose experience is essentially theoretical. Mr Williams has been managing substantial sums of institutional money, specialising in smaller companies, longer than almost anyone else in the UK stock market. And investing, like business in general, is a vocation which cannot be undertaken in the classroom: you need to actually execute real decisions regarding which stocks to buy and sell, and take risks with hard cash. Only then is a genuine track record accumulated, and only then does one truly acquire the experience necessary to forge a great investor.

The author is a serious student of economics, markets and companies, and his book reflects that propensity. His belief in the future of AIM is backed up by sensible observations and research. He points out that AIM is almost the only significant exchange which offers investors access to true microcap stocks, and that it has withstood a decade or so when such shares were largely ignored by institutional investors. They have switched virtually all their attention and activity towards larger capitalisation companies, and diversified internationally across exchanges around the world.

But the credit excesses of recent decades may well mean that overall economic growth is sluggish in coming times, as debt is repaid. And large companies are likely to find that an advancing top line during such conditions is almost impossible. By contrast, smaller companies tend to be better at retaining their vitality, despite near stagnation in the overall economy. The author provides several compelling reasons for this outperformance. Firstly, the Law of Large Numbers militates against giant corporations; secondly, they tend to become increasingly bureaucratic and complex as they expand; thirdly, they lack flexibility and fail to adapt to changes; fourthly they are often poor at embracing innovation; and finally, over time, well established companies are simply more likely to decay, given that companies, like people, tend to have natural life cycles.

I agree with all of these points. I have spent my career taking small companies and attempting to grow them substantially. From PizzaExpress in the 1990s, which we took from a market value of £20m to over £500m, to Integrated Dental Holdings, through to Topps Tiles, Strada, Patisserie Valerie, Giraffe and Gail's, I have always been excited by the prospects of dynamic companies that have the potential to become many times bigger. It is certainly possible to make large sums of money by utilizing financial engineering to boost returns from large, mature companies: that is what the big private equity shops do when they undertake management buyouts. But I prefer the excitement of taking a small brand and seeing it grow two, five, ten or even twentyfold over five to ten years.

Big companies mostly have to grow by acquisition. Generally this delivers worse results than organic growth. Meanwhile smaller companies are often led by founders, or entrepreneurs who have substantial shareholdings. Typically these are highly motivated individuals who in some circumstances are capable of delivering extraordinary value to backers. Such driven men and women like AIM because shares on it qualify for entrepreneurs' relief and relief from inheritance tax.

I've found that in many cases there are diseconomies of scale, with margins falling as a company gets larger. And Mr Williams' book discusses an interesting study which suggests that productivity falls in firms with over 250 employees. All these factors may combine to deliver what is known as the small company effect, whereby nimble microcap stocks can produce better returns than big company shares. Moreover you are more likely to find neglected gems on AIM, since the vast majority of analysts focus almost exclusively on big companies – meaning many small stocks are overlooked.

It could be argued that AIM is high risk, and that stocks on it are illiquid – but as someone principally involved in buying private companies, I am used to that. If you pick the right portfolio of stocks, then the rewards will outweigh the downsides. I also believe that smaller, newer companies are vital for our national interest: they create the large majority of new jobs. So I am pleased that the London Stock Exchange is rediscovering its purpose and raising capital for new issues. I have shown commitment to AIM myself this year by taking public Patisserie Holdings. I believe there are plenty of other businesses out there that will choose to float in the coming year or two, giving private investors the opportunity to buy shares.

All in all therefore, I am delighted to have been asked to write a foreword to *The Future is Small*. Do your homework, remember to diversify – and enjoy the adventure of AIM.

Luke Johnson, September 2014

Acknowledgements

It is always a pleasure to write the acknowledgements, but it is particularly so in this case, because it demonstrates so convincingly how the weaknesses of an individual – me – can be so well-disguised by the complementary strengths of others; a small team of individuals whose skills and enthusiastic engagement brings a book that would never have existed otherwise, together, as it is here.

Mary Ziegler, who has so many other commitments, agreed right from the start to take on writing the book with me. But she has done so much more, tracking down the source material, liaising with all sorts of academic and commercial organisations to ensure they were entirely happy with the use of their content, coordinating with those at Miton, my company, and Harriman House. This book is truly the result of her steady focus on the text and wide-ranging ability to juggle 101 other aspects simultaneously. Mary, many, many thanks for your unstinting help with *The Future is Small*.

Stephen Taylor has also been in from the start. Often ideas, especially financial arguments, can appear dense and unappetising. Stephen brings these alive with images right from the cover onwards, illustrating the key thoughts so that they are accessible at a glance. He is brilliant at this. Enthusiastic and hard-working. You can see for yourself in the following pages. My particular thanks to Stephen too.

The whole thesis of this book sits upon the shoulders of academic giants. It is their work over the last 30 years that has provided the real insight as to the key aspects that really do drive share prices, separate from so many others that are rather more prosaic. In particular I would like to thank the Emeritus Professors from London Business School, Elroy Dimson and Paul Marsh, ably assisted by Mike Staunton, who very generously read several drafts of the book, and raised questions that hadn't been addressed. Professor Ibbotson's recent work from Yale School of Management is groundbreaking too, with his team exploring the linkages between market liquidity and return.

I have also received great encouragement and assistance from a host of professional friends. Luke Johnson of Risk Capital Partners knows first-hand the thrills and challenges of working with genuinely small companies; I am immensely grateful for his views set out in the foreword. Other professional comment has come from Tim Ward, CEO of the Quoted Companies Alliance, and Marcus Stuttard and Umerah Akram of the AIM exchange. Will Wallis of Numis Securities also deserves recognition for his swift responses to queries over the minutiae of research. When it comes to the publication itself, the dedication of the team at Harriman House led by Myles Hunt, and the insistence on clarity from my editor Chris Parker, have all helped to ease the progression of ideas. I am grateful to them all.

Amongst my professional guides for this book are many of my colleagues at Miton Group plc. We have a team of fund managers who have brought new insights, including Martin Turner, Georgina Hamilton, and George Godber. Oliver Bainbridge, who worked for several weeks with us during a university break, and Shayan Mahinfar also provided some helpful comment. In addition I have had wonderful support from Ian Chimes who heads up sales and marketing at Miton and Mark Harper who heads up marketing. They have read and re-read the text, and been ceaselessly supportive, raising matters of substance along with questions of detail. Further comments have come from our equity trader Niall Coyne, and Ian Dighé, the chairman. However, I would like to emphasise that all the judgments about the final content are mine. Miton Group plc has no financial interest in or editorial control over this book whatsoever. Any errors or omissions are entirely my own.

Finally, my thanks should also go to all those who work hard at the thousands and thousands of smaller quoted companies. Without them, there wouldn't be any opportunities for our savings to work hard to generate attractive returns. Working in a smaller company can often be stressful, with most feeling isolated and alone at times. Even those who do work hard sometimes find their efforts have been in vain as the business fails through an abrupt change in the market that is no fault of theirs. Our greatest thanks should go to this multitude of individuals who get far too little praise and recognition.

Gervais Williams, September 2014

Contents

Illustrations

CHAPTER 1

An Age of Confusion

Confusion

1. Uncertainty over what is happening, intended or required.
2. A situation of panic or disorder
3. A disorderly jumble

Oxford Dictionaries

Borrowing growth from the future

Something intriguing happens when you ask a man who's just placed a bet about his chances of winning. His outlook becomes just a little more optimistic than the person still waiting in the queue to hand over his money.[1] This increased confidence in our recent decisions is a fundamental driver in life, in business and in investment. It helps us move on, rather than becoming stuck in the past. But it's worrying because it can blind us to changes in trends.

The financial markets are currently going through a major adjustment. At times like this, data is inconsistent and the world can appear more confusing than ever. In the face of it, most of us prefer to hold on to the trends of the past: to trust in the inevitability of

---

1   Knox, R.E. and Inkster, J.A. (1968), 'Post-decision dissonance at post time', *Journal of Personality and Social Psychology*, 8, pp.319–323. Cited by Wilson, G. (2013), 'The Psychology of Money', lecture at Gresham College, London.

globalisation, awaiting a resurgence of growth that will help the over-indebted to recover once again. This is a comforting vision. It essentially means not deviating from what we know – the established patterns of recent decades.

The problem is, reality itself is deviating from those patterns.

Despite interest rates being held at record low levels, governments running sizeable budget deficits and using huge amounts of quantitative easing (QE), worldwide economic growth has almost ground to a halt. Something big is happening. Something seriously sobering. For decades we've borrowed growth from the future, but that's now coming to an end.

And if current trends are reaching their natural limit, what happens next? How can investors position for the change? This book explores this conundrum, and comes to some controversial conclusions.

Economic life is dominated by concentrations of power; in the corporate world, new technologies have enabled an immense scaling up over the last century. This shift towards supersizing is a trend that's been almost impossible to miss, seeping into many aspects of our lives. The corporate aspects of scale are the focus of this book. And after years when gigantism has been a dominant theme, it seems that we've passed a critical turning point. It's remarkably inconvenient for those businesses and investors obsessed with bigness, because the future is small.

Debt in context

At sustainable levels, nearly everyone agrees that the use of extra finance is overwhelmingly positive – without finance, countries are poor, they stay poor and businesses can't grow.[2] Without finance, families can't buy permanent homes. But in the last 30 years, something alarming has happened. Reliance on debt to drive growth has intensified, with many developed economies moving into a zone where borrowing commitments are vast.

---

2   Ibid.

The scale of the
credit boom

The scale of the credit boom
US credit market debt 1929–2013

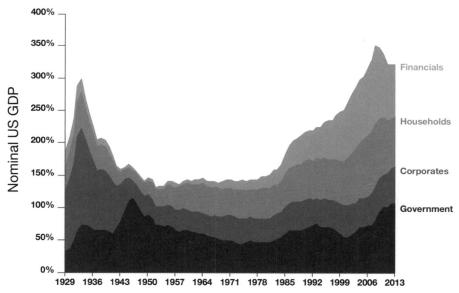

Source: Morgan Stanley Research/Bloomberg/International Monetary Fund/USDA

Take a look at this chart of US credit relative to nominal GDP. A quick check shows two significant peaks. Two bubbles of debt. The first reflects the period of readjustment following the economic imbalances that built up prior to 1929. There were all sorts of ructions that followed during the 1930s. This period of economic adjustment caused great hardship, but financial stability was achieved again after the Second World War. US debt *did* grow after that point, but only in line with GDP. For around 40 years after 1945, the US economy enjoyed a sustained period of prosperity.

But a change of pace took place again in the mid-1980s. Deregulation increased the supply of debt, and as debt increased, so did asset appreciation. This broad rise in asset prices offered capital gains, and those who borrowed to buy more made greater gains. Speculators prospered over the prudent. The trend was progressively reinforced in an intensifying feedback loop. This created a super-sized credit boom that lasted for decades, making up the second peak in the chart.[3]

True, there were scares along the way. There were fears that the collapse of the giant leveraged fund Long-Term Capital Management would drag markets down in 1998. There was the sell-off that followed the dotcom boom in 2000 and the alarming economic stall triggered by worries about the viability of the entire financial system in 2008. After each of these events, markets subsequently recovered and returns were good again, as if nothing very much had changed.

But it has. Commitments to borrow and repay debt can't grow faster than income indefinitely. The boom in mortgage credit that caused problems in 2007 and 2008 has been followed by a boom in government credit.[4] Measures taken by central banks around the world to suppress the cost of borrowing have triggered a surge in issuance of corporate debt[5] as companies seek to take advantage of exceptionally low interest rates. Reliance on debt is greater than ever. **But the credit fix appears to be becoming less and less effective.** Even with additional debt, which at a global level is now 40% higher than in mid-2007,[6] with QE running at full bore and with interest rates at historic lows, world growth is paltry.

We have a problem.

This latest credit boom has been vast.[7] Scaling up – circulating more capital, drawing on ever-more complex financial instruments – has been its distinctive feature. Let's remind ourselves just how much asset values have changed. Back in 1985, the average price of a house in the UK was just over £33,000. By the end of 2007, it had increased more than fivefold to £183,000. By mid-2014, that price topped £186,000.[8]

---

3   Quantitative easing (QE) is not making a difference to government debt in this chart. For every dollar of US assets purchased, the Fed is issuing new dollar deposits. Net net QE is not increasing the accumulated debt in the system.

4   'Global debt exceeds $100tn as governments binge, BIS says', *Bloomberg*, 9 March 2014. Note that the chart shows US liabilities alone, where the shrinking of bank balance sheets has more than offset the increase in government and corporate debt.

5   Hunt, A. (2014), 'The Threat of Deflation Returns – The New Battle for Price Stability', Andrew Hunt Economics.

6   *Bloomberg*, 9 March 2014. Reference incorporates Bloomberg and BIS data, covering sovereign and corporate borrowing.

7   Securitisation (the pooling of assets prior to restructuring and onward selling) might lead to some double counting, but the overall trend is clear.

8   Nationwide House Price Index, real prices non-seasonally adjusted from the UK All-Property series. June 2014.

2013
$100 trillion

Global debt
explodes

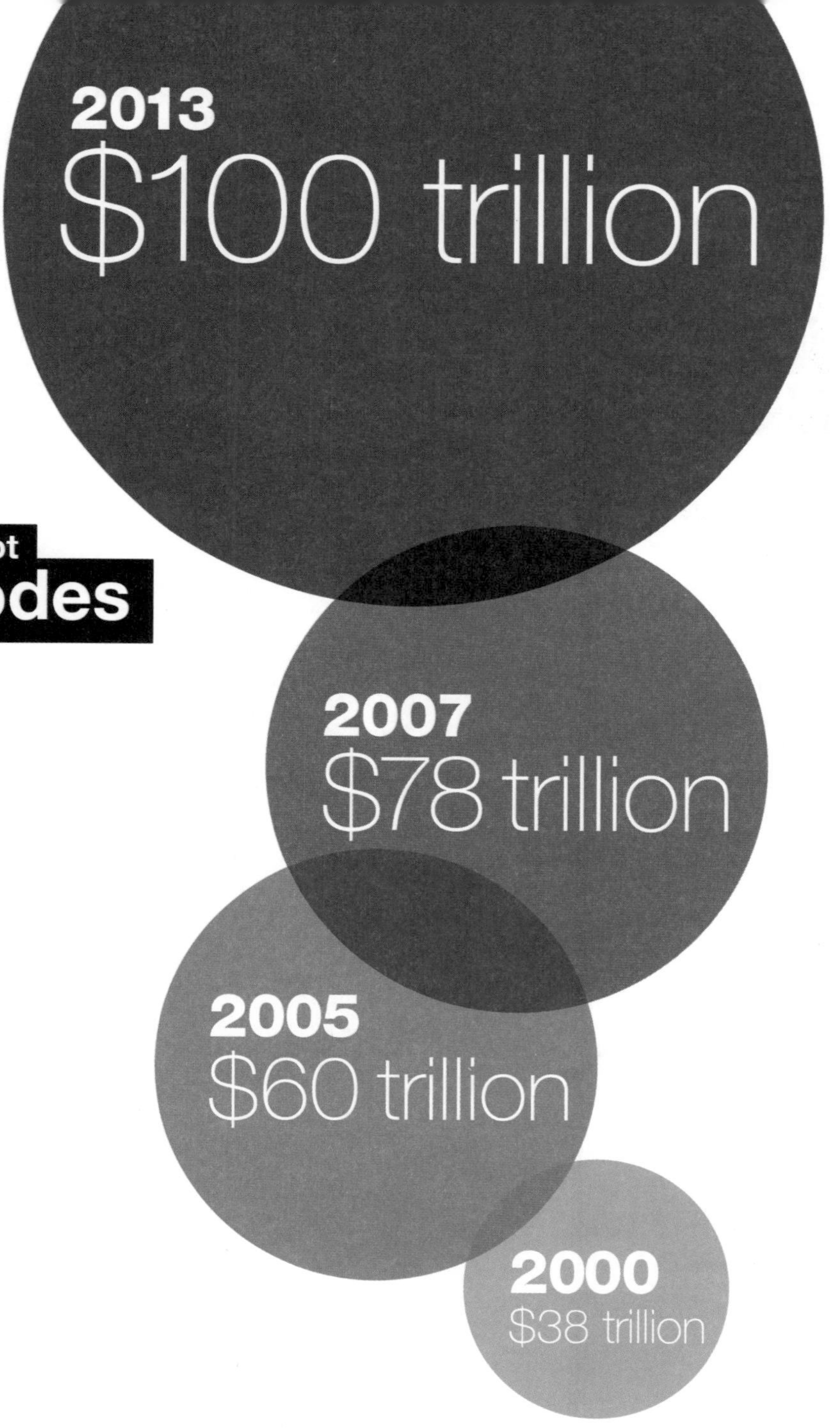

2007
$78 trillion

2005
$60 trillion

2000
$38 trillion

Source: BIS, IMF, incorporating international and domestic debt securities. *BIS Quarterly Review*, March 2014

Other asset prices have risen sharply too. Bonds, commodities, classic cars, fine art, vintage wine have all enjoyed the most extraordinary price appreciation. As the cost of debt is low, many investors continue to borrow to buy more assets if they are in a position to do so, fuelling the feedback cycle. There is an abundance of speculative, secured investment, where the capital borrowed can only be repaid *if asset prices keep rising.*[9]

The UK housing bubble

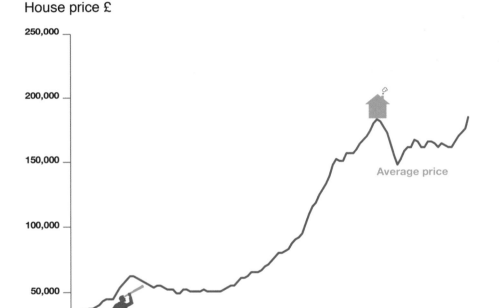

House price £

Source: Nationwide, Office for National Statistics 2014

---

9   Turner, A. (2014), 'Escaping the Debt Addiction: Monetary & Macro-Prudential Policy in the Post-Crisis World', Center for Financial Studies.

Living in a deleveraging world

So what happens in the aftermath of a vast credit bubble? Rather than making assumptions, it's helpful to look back to those who have lived through the ups – and inevitable downs – of these periods before. They have the advantage of being able to stand back and see whole cycles in context.

One of the clearest analyses is now more than 80 years old and comes from Irving Fisher, who drew his evidence from the downturns that began in 1837, 1873 and 1929. After a period of market euphoria in which borrowers overextended themselves, he saw how there was a rush to sell assets once prices began to fall, flooding the market. As so many asset holders all wanted to sell simultaneously, values fell precipitously, with profound implications.

Fisher highlighted that once debt exceeds a critical threshold, there is a self-reinforcing instability where "the more the economic boat tips, the more it tends to tip". That's why the first peak on the debt chart in the illustration on page 3 ('The scale of the credit boom') actually occurs after 1929 – not on the dot of the credit bubble ending, but a little later. In the 1930s there came an alarming collapse of confidence and a downward spiral of falling asset prices, bankruptcy and unemployment. This all led to a reduction in GDP that fell faster than the amount of outstanding debt, so the ratio of debt to GDP actually *increased* for a period after the cycle turned.

Policy actions since 2008 have been raging against something very similar. This time, financial authorities have sought to avoid the policy errors of the past. They have sought to control the cycle and to *reflate* debt-sensitive areas of the economy to inhibit a chaotic downswing in asset prices. By injecting liquidity with QE, and through using ultra-low (and even negative)[10] interest rates, they have prevented a 'worst-case' scenario. In the process, new responsibilities have been taken on; central banks have seriously extended the degree to which they are prepared to intervene in financial markets.

---

10   As pursued in some form by Sweden, Denmark, Switzerland and the European Central Bank.

What happens next?

The aftermath of a vast credit bubble

"Just as a bad cold leads to pneumonia, so over-indebtedness leads to deflation"
Irving Fisher, Econometrica, 1933

I. Mild Gloom and **Shock to Confidence**, Slightly Reduced Velocity of Circulation, Debt Liquidation   II. Money Interest on Safe Loans Falls But Money Interest on Unsafe Loans Rises   III. Distress Selling, More **Gloom**, Fall in Security Prices, More Liquidation, Fall in Commodity Prices   IV. Real Interest Rises; **REAL DEBTS INCREASE**, More Pessimism and Distrust, More Liquidation, More Distress Selling, More Reduction in Velocity   V. More Distress Selling, Contraction of Deposit Currency, Further Dollar Enlargement   VI. Reduction in Net Worth, Increase in **Bankruptcies**, More Pessimism and Distrust, More **Liquidation**   VII. Decrease in Profits, Increase in Losses, Increase in Pessimism, Slower Velocity, More Liquidation **Reduction in Volume of Stock Trading**   VIII. Decrease in Construction, Reduction in Output, Reduction in Trade, Unemployment, More **Pessimism**   IX. Hoarding   X. Runs on Banks, Banks Curtailing Loans for Self-Protection, Banks Selling Investments, **Bank Failures**, Distrust Grows, More Hoarding, More Liquidation, More Distress Selling, Further Dollar Enlargement

Source: Fisher, I (1933), 'The Debt-Deflation Theory of Great Depressions', *Econometrica*, 1, IV

These measures have resulted in a growing list of new abbreviations – ZIRPs, NIRPs, TLTROs and so on[11] – almost a whole new language for the post-crisis world. The measures have been both more successful and less successful than might have been hoped. More successful because the period of adjustment has been extended, and some vicious feedback loops have been tempered. As a by-product of these policies, some assets – like shares – have been given a shot of adrenaline. But their apparent success hides the fact that many of the fault lines remain in place. In particular, underlying attitudes are broadly unchanged and policy actions continue to mask the scale of the imbalances that are still to be unwound.

QE – involving the electronic creation of money which is then used to buy financial assets – is particularly distorting. This once-radical policy, designed to improve the flow in the financial system, has been used extensively by central banks. Whilst it has revitalised capital markets, some of which have surged back to new peaks, it is failing to increase the productive capacity of our economies. There's plenty of capital available, but real investment – investment in new capacity to produce goods and services more competitively – remains at very low levels. Indeed, some argue that QE is indirectly crowding out productive investment. In revitalising capital markets quite so thoroughly, it's allowed parts of the financial sector to remain removed from the realities of life in the rest of the economy. And of course, as a side effect, it has tilted the scales in favour of those who already own assets.

All the while, many of the features identified by Fisher and set out in the illustration 'What happens next?' have been witnessed or are beginning to be evident around the world to varying degrees. But for now QE is contributing to the normalisation myth, helping to promote the notion that the credit boom problems will be resolved without any significant change of behaviour.

Scale of the forthcoming change

Having steered around the major financial risks of 2007 and 2008, the current ambition of governments and central banks appears to be to manage the wind-down of indebtedness through dilution via renewed economic growth. In other words, to wait for economic momentum to pick up again, enabling the servicing of debt to continue and the gradual

---

11   ZIRP: zero interest rate policy, NIRP: negative interest rate policy, TLTRO: targeted long-term refinancing operation.

reduction of borrowing commitments. If all goes to plan, this will allow our over-indebted economies to move out of the danger zone eventually.

However, despite massive stimulus, world growth remains disappointing. In fact, it's been so disappointing that some economists are starting to talk about something odd going on.[12] Demand has been subdued, growth has not bounced back as fast as might be expected and unemployment has been stubbornly hard to shift. It has brought back some unsettling memories of Japan in the 1990s, a nation that fell into a post-boom slump lasting decades. Indeed, some economies, such as the UK, have become *less* efficient since 2007. On average, Britain now produces less each hour, while life expectancy is increasing. Together these trends place extra pressure on the working population. The implications for future prosperity are serious.

During the boom years, we were effectively borrowing growth from the future. Now we're in a period of growth hangover, with growth rates likely to be sub-normal for an extended period.[13] Take a look at the 'The scale of the credit boom' illustration again. The excesses of our most recent credit boom are vast. **The latest peak is around twice or even three times the size of the previous credit boom in 1929**, when the willingness to take on extra debt reached its former limit. Even with aggressive policies in the 1930s, it took more than 15 years for the 1929 excesses to be unwound. So it would be surprising if the excesses of the recent credit boom – one larger in scale and addressed with policies that have stretched out the adjustment period – were resolved in 30 years. Recoveries from financial crises are notoriously slow – this one will take decades.

The disadvantages of speculation

When asset prices have been rising, it's been easy to believe that successful investment relies upon buying cheaply and selling on at a decent profit to someone else who just has an even more optimistic view of the future. After a credit boom lasting over 25 years, there are few who believe that successful investing means anything else.

But this kind of transactional investment, which seeks rapid and lucrative payoffs on a frequent basis, suffers from a fatal weakness. The investor's return is heavily reliant on timing. If the purchase is made at a time when asset prices are low, and the sale is made

---

12   See the speech given by the former US Treasury Secretary Lawrence Summers at the IMF Economic Forum, Washington DC, 8 November 2013.

13   Reinhart, C.M. and Rogoff, K.S. (2009), *This Time is Different* (Princeton University Press).

at a time when asset prices are higher, then the investment return will be attractive. But there's no law that asset prices always rise, let alone on cue. What happens if they don't? It's worth reflecting on the fact that since the end of 1999 the level of the FTSE 100 index has hardly risen at all.

Those employing such transactional strategies have been finding it increasingly difficult to make the kind of returns they were accustomed to. Since the full frenzy of the credit boom during the mid-2000s, stock market volumes have fallen. Many professionals are finding it harder to deal freely, even in the stocks of the most actively traded, larger quoted companies. The patterns of the markets have changed. Low-volatility income stocks have led the stock market rally between the middle of 2011 and the end of 2013 rather than the high-beta[14] speculative stocks that used to lead the way when markets recovered.

All this shows that we are now entering a period when asset prices might not rally politely as they have in the past. The full implications of this have just been veiled by stimulative measures in the short term. If this is the case, then transactional strategies are unlikely to succeed. And when asset prices stagnate, it becomes self-evident that transactional investors play a zero-sum game. Those who successfully trade for a profit can only do so at the price of someone else incurring a similar loss on the market. Some can fight those kinds of odds and succeed, but the maths means that most cannot. Successful investment will need to be based upon deeper foundations.

For these reasons, it is unwise to use asset prices as the only measure of wealth creation. Clearly asset prices are an *indication* of current valuations. But current valuations change all the time. And sometimes they adjust downwards in giant steps, such as those witnessed during 2008, so they are not an especially resilient measure of progress. They are essentially temporal.

More tangible assets are better yardsticks of real wealth. The best of these tend to have a physical presence, with perhaps the best example being land. The wealth of some of the most prosperous families in the UK and many of the colleges of Oxford and Cambridge is based upon long-term land holdings. Land is an asset of real duration that has sustained wealth through world wars, periods of economic depression, currency crises, financial crises and periods of inflation. Clearly there is value in the property on the land, too, though with changes in utility or suitability its value can decay over time. Other assets with a physical presence include precious metals. Most investors have a relatively modest

---

14   Beta: measure of volatility in relation to the market as a whole.

proportion of their savings in land or precious metals, though many hold buildings where prices have risen significantly during the boom.

Aside from residential property, most savings are held collectively in rather less tangible assets – in share certificates, loans to corporations and governments or in unitised funds.[15] Essentially all of these savings are indirect holdings that look through to the value of more tangible assets further up the chain. Investors in unitised funds look through to the value of the equities held on their behalf, and ultimately the value of those individual equities is reliant upon the success of those businesses in delivering products or services that are valuable to the wider public.

The linkage between the saver and the ultimate home of those savings in a quoted company has become more tenuous during the credit boom, when transactional strategies have become more popular. For many, the key feature when choosing an investment has been the potential for its price to rise. Will Chinese stock market indices rise, or is it better to back an ETF that rises twice as fast at the FTSE 100? Relatively little thought is given to the ultimate foundations of the asset price or the real wealth on which it is founded. This is now changing. This change in attitude is going to shape markets beyond the boom as investors start to take a much closer interest in how their own savings are put to work.

Conclusion

The scale of the credit overhang is enormous. The total volume of debt that's been issued may not fade away quietly, particularly if world growth continues to disappoint. Although strong deflationary forces may have been contained for now, the unwinding of the excesses of the boom is going to be demanding for everyone.

As market trends change, some of the assumptions that have underpinned our understanding of the most effective ways in which to invest are going to be challenged. Currently, the allocation of our collective savings, in pension schemes and pooled funds, reflects the themes of the past. But these market trends are reliant on debt continuing to rise, which quite clearly conflicts with systemic constraints. This is a good time to review what has been driving current trends and to start considering how they might change. How the future might be different is exactly what this book seeks to explore.

---

15   Unitised fund: collective savings vehicle which allows the pooling of funds.

CHAPTER 2

How Bigness Came to Dominate

Questions of scale

In the buoyant decades prior to 2007, upscaling was the dominant trend. The 'big consensus' encouraged concentrations of economic power[16] and an innovative and deregulated financial industry helped companies to grow. But before delving more deeply into what we know about how very large organisations function and their appeal for investors, let's check what size means for quoted companies.

On the surface, it seems quite obvious that there's a difference between large and small – but the precise boundaries are ambiguous. Size is relative, and there's just no single definition as to what defines a small or 'micro-cap' company in comparison to mid-scale or large. However, if corporate scale is going to become increasingly important for investors in the coming years – the main thesis of this book – it's important to understand the differences, to understand which stocks are likely to benefit and which might lose out.

Let's take a look at some different benchmarks of stock-market smallness which vary considerably across the globe. In the US, any company that's not large enough to be part of the Russell 2000 index is considered ultra-small or, in our terminology, micro cap. In 2014, the Russell 2000 index covered companies valued between approximately £100m

16   See the debate by Lent, A. (2014), 'Small is Powerful: Escaping the 20th century love of big power', RSA, 15 June 2014.

to £1.9bn.[17] Japan also has a complex and vibrant smaller company sector. The Jasdaq Standard index had a lower boundary of smallness close to the £50m mark in 2014, while the members of the Jasdaq Growth and Mothers indices include more diminutive companies.[18] Move to Europe, and 'small' means something larger than in the US. The widely used Euro Stoxx Small index is typically made up of stocks valued around £800m to £2.8bn.[19] Most professionally managed funds that invest in smaller companies tend to invest in companies of this kind of scale.

In the UK, our definitions of small are different again. The FTSE SmallCap index encompasses companies valued between around £50m to £600m,[20] while those in the FTSE Fledgling index[21] would be regarded as micro-sized. Yet even this is not quite the whole story. There is also another benchmark of smallness in the UK – the Numis Smaller Companies Index (NSCI),[22] set up in 1987. NSCI's universe includes the smallest 10% of companies by value listed on the London Stock Exchange (LSE). But since the index was established more than two decades ago, the boundary between 'small' and 'mid-sized' or 'larger' has moved up from £100m to close to £1,500m![23]

Why? Well the Alternative Investment Market (AIM) was established in 1995 as London's junior market, specifically designed to make it easier for smaller businesses to have a listing. Since then, many smaller quoted companies have chosen to move their listing from the mainstream LSE to AIM. Most new smaller company flotations have taken place on AIM, which has slightly different listing requirements from the main market. As a result, and as stock markets have risen, the boundary between small and large has migrated upwards. The appreciation of larger quoted stocks has vastly increased the overall value of those quoted on the LSE and therefore the value range of each stock market decile. Secondly, with fewer smaller quoted companies listed on the LSE, many that were included in the calculation in 1987 are now excluded because they are listed on AIM.

---

17   Russell 2000 index: a US benchmark index made up of the 2000 smallest stocks by market capitalisation of the Russell 3000 index. This is the industry benchmark for US smallcap stocks. Russell Indices, as at rebalancing May 2013. Lowest and highest stock market capitalisation between $168m and $3.1bn respectively.

18   Jasdaq Indices. Listed company information. As at October 2013.

19   Stoxx Factsheet, as at March 2014. Lowest and highest stock market capitalization €1bn and €3.5bn respectively.

20   FTSE Group, as at September 2014.

21   FTSE Fledgling index: index constructed from UK stocks too small to be included in the FTSE All-Share.

22   Formerly the Hoare Govett Smaller Companies index (HGSC).

23   Dimson, E. and Marsh, P. (2014), *Numis Smaller Companies Index Annual Review 2014* (Numis Securities).

The changes in the LSE market, along with the effects of inflation, mean that lots of mid-sized stocks are included in main market definitions of 'small'. This is important. *Fewer really tiny, ant-sized companies appear in the smallest 10% of companies listed on the LSE than used to be the case.*

At the other extreme, among the ranks of over 1,000 companies listed on the AIM exchange are many valued at less than £50m.[24] This is absolutely a market where it's possible to access the genuinely small company. When broken down by cap size, the largest cohort of AIM quoted stocks are those with market capitalisations in the £10m to £50m range.[25] This breadth of smallness is remarkable. However, because AIM-listed companies are not included in mainstream benchmarks such as the FTSE All-Share index, these stocks are often considered off-piste from an institutional point of view.

How small is small?

The key point is that the UK's heritage of corporate smallness is rather different to other countries'. Remember that most international smaller company indices have higher cut-offs; the UK has a wider-ranging universe of the smallest quoted stocks. Why does it matter? It's important because corporate smallness has some distinctive characteristics – in particular, smaller companies have the ability to retain vitality in the face of sluggish economic conditions. Not all of them, of course, but enough to differentiate them from significantly larger businesses. This is a feature that this book will explore. But, as stock markets have appreciated in recent years, and as markets themselves have evolved, some mid-sized companies have become classified as 'small' within some smaller company indices. This factor has led to a degree of ambiguity as to what really defines a smaller company in investment terms. Various smaller company indices seem to include constituents that used to be regarded as large.

So there are no tidy, universal definitions of smallness. Smaller listed companies might employ over 1,000 people. But micro-sized businesses – such as the ant-sized companies listed on AIM – are probably closer to a layman's view of what small really means, and the ones this book argues are most interesting from an investment perspective. We'll return to this in Chapter 5.

---

24   AIM Factsheet, April 2014.
25   *Ibid.*

How small is small?

Smallest stock in various equity indices around the world

Smallest listed company by market capitalisation

UK Numis Smaller Companies Index* <1m

UK FTSE AIM All-Share* <1m

*Indices include all smaller UK
quoted companies, with no lower
market capitalisation boundary

UK FTSE SmallCap
£47 million

USA Russell 2000 Index
£100 million

EU
£

Source: Russell Investments, Euro Stoxx, FTSE Group, Numis Securities, LSE Sterling equivalent, as at last rebalancing

ROPE

C915 n

Euro Stoxx Small Index

Some disadvantages of bigness

When it comes to corporate scale, there are sizeable problems with bigness. Gigantic scale and vibrant growth don't usually go hand in hand.

The larger a company becomes, the mightier it becomes within its own markets. So larger companies tend to have larger market shares than smaller companies. Some see this as an advantage: those with major brands and established access to markets can launch new products more quickly than peripheral players. When Unilever and the like launch a new product, they can get it in front of millions of consumers fast. They have strong and established relationships with global retailers and can afford to advertise the arrival of their new products widely.

But there's a simple problem with larger market shares: there's not much scope for winning significantly more in the future. In other words, larger companies find it hard to expand at a rate that exceeds that of the market. And when markets peak and suffer a downturn, larger companies with their larger market shares have little scope to offset the wider trend. So larger businesses have the major disadvantage that their prospects tend to become constrained by the Law of Large Numbers. This law, based on a key principle in probability theory, suggests that as a sample grows, its mean will move closer to the average in its own particular context. Translated into the corporate world, this suggests that maintaining above-trend growth will become increasingly difficult as a company expands, as the challenge to grow expands too. The bigger a business, the less scope there is for it to grow.

And there are other problems with scale too. We know them quite instinctively. Larger companies, for instance, tend to become more bureaucratic. Initially that disadvantage is offset by greater buying power, which tends to keep costs down. But the larger a company becomes, the more internal processes are needed to coordinate the different parts of the whole. As larger companies widen operations across a number of markets, they become more and more complex to manage, leaving employees grappling with fragmented information. It seems obvious that a handful of units, physically close, might be easier to manage than a number of larger, potentially more diverse and perhaps more geographically dispersed ones. This issue emerged very clearly after 2008 when the risks being taken within outsized financial organisations were shown to be much greater than those perceived by their management teams.[26]

---

26   Power, M., Ashby, S. and Palermo, T. (2013), *Risk Culture in Financial Organisations: Final Report* (Financial Services Knowledge Transfer Network).

And ultimately, there is decay. Over time, as businesses expand and mature, the vibrancy within an organisation can be lost. Internal processes tend to calcify. A company becomes less able to respond to market change. Ultimately larger companies become so unwieldy that they start to decline and collapse from the inside. Former giants find that their markets are lost to newer, more flexible competitors; there are numerous examples of occasions when large, established incumbents have failed to spot potential within the tiny seeds of new ideas.

Indeed, there are so many natural problems with unbridled scale, it's worth asking why it's become such a cult in recent decades. Why is largeness so appealing in the corporate world, and why have the equity portfolios of sophisticated fund managers become almost universally aligned with size?

Controlling risk bandwidth
Understanding scale

ORGANISATION
A

← ASPIRED →

← ACTUAL →

Source: Developed from Astbury, S., Palermo, T. and Power, M. (2012), *Risk culture in financial organisations: An interim report* (London School of Economics)

The pull towards scale during the credit boom

Most trends are explained by simple human characteristics. In a complex world, we naturally prefer shortcuts to subtleties. Shades of grey fail to command attention when simple classification is so much easier. For speed and ease, we categorise. Large or small, like or dislike, and so on. The radical economist Schumacher wrote about this;[27] it's not new. Yet over the last two or three decades, scale has come to predominate. During the most recent credit boom, there were particular advantages of scale.

In the boom, the UK economy grew at a premium pace, and so did other markets around the world. The international agreements under the General Agreement on Tariffs and Trade (GATT) and later the World Trade Organisation (WTO) radically changed the global economy. They enhanced growth by opening the way for a flood of imports from lesser-developed economies into developed western markets. As the world economy became more connected, consumers were able to buy goods produced more cheaply – much more cheaply – from outside the UK.

Whilst this might have enhanced UK growth overall, it came at a price. Many existing UK suppliers suffered, including both smaller and larger businesses. However, larger companies operating across several economies were able to offset any lost volume in their home markets with extra volume from their overseas operations. Particular advantages came for those with the largest reach, operating in the least-developed economies, since their greater access to lower-cost production meant they were best-placed to take extra market share.

At times of growth, those with the best access to funding are also best-placed to take advantage of opportunities. And larger, well-established companies tend to enjoy easier and cheaper access to capital. In the most recent credit boom, they have been able to take full advantage of their cheaper access to capital in developed markets and apply that advantage to the rapid growth opportunities within emerging economies, further enhancing their growth rates.

One of the notable features of the UK economy is the scale of its engagement with others around the world. The growth of international trade is good for the UK and London dominates international currency trading. The UK's imperial history means that its financial links with many developing markets are well-established and have lasted for years. Once the credit boom really gained momentum in the mid-1990s, London grew to become one of the largest financial centres in the world. The scale effects of growth

---

27   Schumacher, E.F. (1973), *Small is Beautiful* (Blond and Briggs), p.54.

plus the benefits of the lower cost of traded goods increased corporate profit margins. This increased the ability of companies to generate cash, and made it easier to fund yet more growth. Share prices soared. The UK enjoyed the longest period of uninterrupted economic growth ever in the run up to 2008.

Those who took on debt early in the boom greatly enhanced their wealth. For example, if a business was wholly funded by shares, and it grew at, say, 10% a year, shareholders benefited at the same rate. However, if the same business funded one half of its capital needs via debt, then the earnings growth on the lesser amount of equity would nearly double. (Remember there would be some interest costs marginally offsetting the extra growth; it's easy to get carried away at times of enthusiasm!) All this encouraged corporates to fund more growth with extra debt. Old-fashioned caution over indebtedness seemed unnecessarily prudent. In a period of falling interest rates, the willingness to use corporate debt simply exploded in scale.

With industrial growth in the use of debt, banks struggled to fund all their opportunities. But fortunately corporate debt was saleable, as it was normally priced at slightly higher interest rates than government bonds. So an exchange was established where banks could sell-on corporate loans to investors so that they could move on and make yet more loans. However, traded corporate bonds needed to be of a reasonable scale to make the listing process worthwhile. So once again those with scale were favoured by this trend.

Banks scaled up, industrialising many of their processes so that loan approvals could keep up with the growth opportunities. In this environment, a single loan for £400m in a large corporate transaction naturally appeared much more 'efficient' than lending £2m to 200 smaller businesses. The cash lent to larger corporates could be sold on. Numerous smaller loans were more problematic. Therefore banks started to favour larger loans and moved to centralise lending decisions, where these larger risks could be monitored more closely. All this degraded the ability of regional bank managers to fund smaller quoted companies. Perversely, in the midst of a credit boom, many smaller quoted companies found their access to credit increasingly constrained.

In the expansionary phase,[28] scale had the advantage again and again. Smaller quoted companies lost out as a result of their greater domestic bias. They lost out because they weren't necessarily well-placed to take advantage of the rapid growth of emerging

---

28   Broadly defined here as the two and a half decades prior to 2008.

markets. And they lost out because their access to debt decreased – let alone being able to take advantage of its falling cost.

The credit boom unambiguously favoured scale.

Professional investment in large and small

Every time someone wishes to borrow to purchase an asset, the relevant lending institution creates a loan on its books. However, elsewhere the individual who agrees to sell that asset gets an equal cash balance in their bank account. And if they do not have a specific use for that capital, it's often handed over to the financial sector to manage. In this way, the recent growth and vast scale of the fund management industry is closely correlated with the credit boom and the associated increase in the value of a wide variety of assets. In 1986, the UK industry managed just over £2.5trn, but that ballooned to £4.5trn over the following two and half decades.[29] Many larger fund management institutions now manage tens or even hundreds of billions of pounds. Their growth in scale, along with the market trends established during the credit boom, have had profound implications for the way in which they invest.

Prior to the mid-1980s, most long-term institutional investors held a decent capital weighting in a wide spread of domestic quoted companies, including those outside the major indices. This diversification helped add resilience to portfolios, as smaller listed companies and those outside the main benchmarks offered access to a rather different mix of industrial opportunities (and thereby risks) compared with the mainstream universe of larger stocks.

But as globalisation and international connectedness have progressed, professional investors have become more international in orientation. Managers have often sought to diversify overseas, where they can participate in the rapid growth of developing markets, in preference to the traditional strategy of investing in smaller companies at home. So portfolio weightings have radically changed over the last 25 years. Nearly all UK quoted companies have seen their institutional shareholder base decline, despite the rapid growth in the scale of capital managed by these institutions. International diversification effectively reduced the need for professional investors to hold UK smaller quoted companies, although they tend to behave rather differently to larger ones.

---

29   Investment Management Association, London.

Financial deregulation accelerated globalisation, and globalisation specifically favoured the large over the small. The majority of smaller companies are just too small to access the corporate bond markets, so they did not participate in debt-funding to the same degree as larger ones. And, in a rather circular way, the smallness of smaller companies became more of an acute problem during the boom as asset managers themselves scaled up. All these factors contributed to the general reduction of professional interest in investing in the smallest UK quoted companies and the progressive withdrawal of institutional capital. Fast forward to 2014 and very little of the capital invested by the largest institutions in the UK is now invested outside the very largest 350 of them.

Investment flows
in and out of UK smaller companies

Total net sales £m

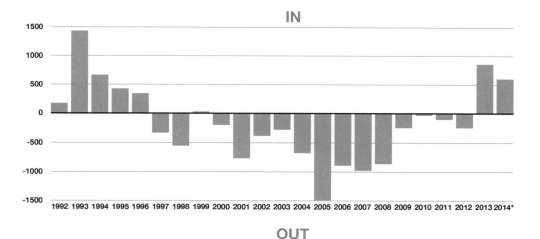

Source: IMA, June 2014; including retail and institutional investment.
*January to May inclusive

The smallest quoted companies have had the cards stacked against them for many reasons. The withdrawal of institutional capital at a time when most others enjoyed increased access to capital completed the perfect storm, ensuring that the returns from the UK index dedicated to smaller companies, the FTSE SmallCap index,[30] have been relatively poor since it was established in 1990.

Remember, during the recent credit boom stock markets rose at an exaggerated pace. The FTSE 100 launched in 1984 at 1000; by 2014 it topped 6800.[31] In the pre-crisis phase, plentiful growth was unremarkable. It was widely accessible in many asset classes, and in both small and large quoted companies. It was available in domestic and international companies, in western developed economies and in rapidly transforming emerging markets. Over time, professional investors began to recognise that they could access ample growth in a more limited equity universe – a universe wholly made up of larger organisations. They could hone their research efforts on the relatively modest number of larger companies, where inspired selections could make a much bigger difference to portfolio returns. Holdings in smaller companies seemed rather troublesome by comparison; being small, even modest positions are difficult to adjust at will. So most institutional investors entirely disengaged from the tiniest companies; the vibrant ants were found to be too small for inclusion. And despite the larger companies' problems with bureaucracy and complexity, the FTSE 100 returns were better than those of the FTSE SmallCap index up to 2011.

During the expansionary period, mid-cap companies[32] outperformed the FTSE 100 by an enormous margin. Many of these companies have the key advantages of largeness – they are multinational in orientation, able to take advantage of the growth of markets outside the UK, and large enough to enhance their growth rates with the use of corporate debt. But they also have the advantage of being smaller and nimbler than the largest companies. So whilst the largest companies have had the advantage of globalisation, mid-cap stocks have had this, plus some of the advantages of a degree of immaturity too. They had better growth potential than the very largest companies. So the mid-sized companies in the FTSE 250 index outperformed both the FTSE 100 and the FTSE SmallCap index by a simply gigantic amount.

---

30   FTSE SmallCap index: UK benchmark made up of companies too small to feature in the cluster of the largest 350 listed companies by market capitalisation. It represents approximately 2% of the total UK market by value.

31   *Thomson Reuters.* The overall return is considerably higher when dividend income is taken into account too.

32   Defined here by the FTSE 250 index, a UK benchmark made up of mid-capitalised companies that fall outside the FTSE 100, representing approximately 15% of the total UK market by value.

The outperformance of the FTSE 250

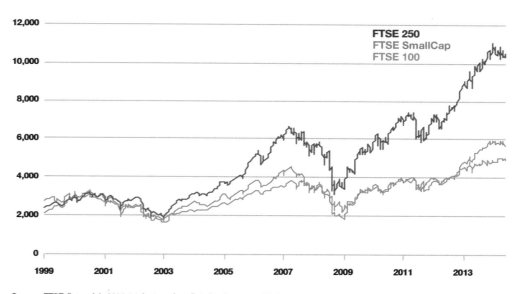

Source: FTSE Group July 2014, total return since first directly comparable inception date

In this context, most institutions see no impetus for changing how they allocate their capital – particularly as the use of artificial stimulus has softened the edges of the credit hangover. They believe that they already have the best of both worlds. They have a collective benchmark index that comprises just 350 companies, so they can focus their research on just one fifth of the stocks quoted in London. They also believe that they have plenty of participation in growth; the mid-cap stocks have the advantage of being more moderate in scale, and therefore being immature to a degree, and not saddled with the same super-sized challenges as the very largest quoted companies.

So corporate bigness now dominates the investment universe of most institutional investors. Few professionals give much consideration to allocating capital to genuinely small quoted companies. The disadvantages of doing so are well understood. Smaller companies are small and fiddly; it's difficult to allocate decent percentages of a portfolio to them. They are illiquid, and during a good part of the credit boom they have proved very difficult to sell. Finally, the FTSE SmallCap index has often underperformed the FTSE 100, and greatly underperformed the FTSE 250 since these indices were first established. Most chief investment officers of institutional investment houses are entirely unconcerned about having little or no investment in the smallest quoted companies.

Conclusion

Investment firms have always been large, but in the past the diversification and performance benefits of smaller companies used to justify their inclusion in most institutional portfolios. Globalisation changed all that. It stimulated institutions to allocate more capital overseas, so the diversification benefits offered by the UK smaller company universe became less important. Secondly, institutional portfolios became more aligned with mainstream benchmark indices, which are naturally dominated by larger quoted companies. Together these factors led most investors to modify their strategies and progressively withdraw institutional capital from the smallest UK quoted companies.

As banks industrialised their lending, the authority of regional bank managers was scaled back, and smaller UK quoted businesses also found it more difficult to borrow during the boom. Alongside the withdrawal of institutional capital from genuinely small quoted companies, this has greatly impeded their ability to invest. Smaller company indices did not perform well during the boom.

The pattern has become so well-established that most institutional investors now believe that they can safely ignore the very smallest quoted companies. After all, genuinely small companies have no part to play when the commercial imperative is to outperform others in portfolios of the largest 350 UK quoted companies. Ant-sized business appear entirely irrelevant to the gigantic scale of financial institutions.

Institutions do worry about how to best position their clients' capital now that world growth is slowing. But increasing weightings in the smallest stocks at a time of economic challenge seems completely perverse. Why take additional risk with market liquidity within portfolios at such a time? Few institutions intend moving away from the consensus.

But they are in for a shock. A sea-change in attitudes towards genuinely small quoted companies is coming, and most market participants are trend followers in the end. Chapter 3 outlines why smaller quoted companies will become much more significant for investors once again in the years ahead.

CHAPTER 3

Unsettling Challenges for the Status Quo

Growth characteristics amongst the big and the small

When growth was plentiful, the advantages of smallness appeared unremarkable. Larger companies grew well in a record-breaking phase of economic expansion up to 2008; for the more adventurous, emerging markets offered supersonic growth. Modern investment strategies also had the advantage of offering investors the ability to allocate capital in great scale, often along with plentiful liquidity too.

Individual smaller businesses, like the luxury bag maker Mulberry, may have performed strongly for a period, but at a time when rapid growth was widely accessible, their performance was still fairly unexceptional in terms of the absolute scale of the gains. And in contrast to larger companies, smaller companies always carry the considerable disadvantage of being small and fiddly. Due to their modest scale, a vast number of individual stocks are needed to make them meaningful in larger portfolios. In a sector dogged by illiquidity, this all seemed like too much trouble to be worth it. During the credit boom, there were many cogent reasons to avoid genuinely small stocks.

But this logic faces new challenges beyond the boom. In the first chapter of this book we highlighted how far the world has been borrowing growth from the future. The second explained why this led to portfolios dominated by larger companies as globalisation progressed. But now it seems that we've entered a different phase – a period of growth hangover – where international growth rates might be sub-normal for an extended period. So it's a perfect time in which to reassess exactly how the growth characteristics of large and small businesses differ. These findings could drive a major change in the way in which institutional capital is allocated in the future.

Growth among smallness

Growth amongst small firms has very distinct differences from growth amongst larger companies. Perhaps most importantly, the growth of smaller companies is less dependent on general economic expansion. In a period when world growth is sub-normal, this is highly relevant. Clearly all businesses tend to trade better at times of economic expansion and less well during recessions – small businesses are no different in this regard. But many small companies have much greater potential to sustain growth even in times of economic stagnation. Their growth prospects are less tied to the overall economic climate and more related to the specific circumstances of the operations within the business itself.

The growth of most larger companies is principally correlated with the overall trend in their markets, mainly because of their dominant market shares. During phases of economic stagnation, growth is elusive. At these times, companies need to take extra market share in order to maintain momentum. The problem is that large companies need to take a *lot* of market share, otherwise the impact is trivial given their large scale. But there are sizeable risks that come from aggressively pursuing market share. Few competitors are willing to cede ground, so it often sparks fierce price competition. This is exactly what has occurred in the UK food retailing market. If you're big, it pays to rein in ambition in flat-lining markets.

In contrast, genuinely small firms can nibble away, taking market share from others without necessarily causing great market disruption. Minor increments of market share may add up to decent growth for a smaller company. And, being small, modestly sized businesses are often early adopters in novel market developments too. Small company entrepreneurs tend to be closer to the coalface and spot new opportunities earlier. After all, new markets are almost always tiny at first, and therefore of less consequence to the immediate growth of larger companies.

So at a time when world growth prospects are sub-normal, the growth potential of a typical small company is somewhat better than that of its larger competitors. When economic growth is limited, the genuinely small can continue to record good levels of growth in a way simply beyond larger businesses. This makes some smaller companies particularly 'anti-fragile', not only able to survive in volatile times but, on occasion, to thrive too.[33]

Convergence and over-optimisation

During the credit boom, the principal market trends became consistent and ingrained over decades. Growth was plentiful, and those that geared up via debt, or those with access to the supernormal growth of emerging markets, often delivered the most. The extraordinary duration of the credit boom led to a convergence of corporate strategies, with the result that many larger companies now have very similar investment characteristics. A quick look at the top 100 companies in the UK reveals how far this has gone. The share prices of most FTSE 100 stocks – and indeed many other asset classes too – tend to move up and down together as the perception of risk ebbs and flows.

As credit boom trends start to tail off and emergency policies are scaled back, the full risks of this convergence will become obvious. Contrary to expectations, emerging markets are far from 'decoupled' from growth in developed markets; very few of them have developed their own growth-drivers that are independent of global trends. Furthermore, in time it seems likely that the huge amounts of corporate bonds issued by the largest companies could become something of millstone for those that have over-optimised[34] their balance sheets.

The risk of over-optimisation amongst larger companies has not been greatly recognised yet. At the time of the global financial crisis, some businesses were over-levered, but the emergency reduction of UK interest rates from 5.75% in 2007 to an historically-low 0.5% in 2009 meant that this challenge didn't necessarily get addressed. In fact, super-low interest rates have simply reinvigorated the corporate debt markets still further. Many companies have taken on extra debt and the extra risks that come with it. As Irving Fisher pointed out, there's now an increased chance that this extra debt will make markets more volatile in the future and ultimately risk a flood of asset sales if interest rates rise more than anticipated.

---

33   Taleb, N.N. (2012), *Antifragile: Things that gain from disorder* (Penguin).
34   Over-optimise: to modify for apparent efficiency but in doing so introduce potential vulnerabilities.

The big problem for many investment institutions is that they have narrowed their investment portfolios into larger UK companies and diversified into similar companies overseas. So these kinds of investment portfolios are doubly exposed. They are dependent on a limited number of stocks in the UK and frequently the larger companies they hold in overseas portfolios operate in similar industries. They too have geared up during the boom. There is a real danger that there is a much higher degree of correlation in institutional portfolios than currently recognised.

Diversity and resilience – an analogy

Diversification is important. In comparison to the ocean-going vessels of the large corporation, smaller companies can be likened to small boats – some are fishing craft, others are lifeboats or racing yachts. When conditions are challenging, most will struggle to some degree. Larger companies are assumed to carry lesser risk, given the advantage of their major brands and sizeable market positions; they may suffer a reduction in sales, but the genuinely small could find certain niches completely blown away. Certainly many more individual small companies are prone to founder and sink at difficult times.

But this overlooks the advantages of smallness. Whilst some *do* fail, others operating in distinctive niches can be particularly well-placed for new challenges. In the shallow seas of a low-growth world, there are bound to be some smaller vessels that are perfectly placed to clean up, whereas the larger drafts of most of the bigger businesses constrict their opportunity. Smaller vessels can head into the lee of an island where conditions are less severe, whereas larger vessels are obliged to stay further offshore in the swell. And during a hurricane it's sometimes safer to be in a virtually unsinkable lifeboat, even if it's tossed aside and inverted by large waves. Large vessels carry lifeboats for just such an eventuality.

The key point is that, in comparison with the limited universe of large companies, there are hundreds of smaller quoted companies for investors to consider. As in a rich and thriving ecosystem, diversity offers resilience, which is particularly valuable at times of challenge. Amongst the wide-ranging smaller company universe, many will find ways to sustain growth in spite of a world where growth is erratic or indeed largely absent.

This is an important consideration for investment portfolios given the challenges ahead. After the boom, most of the larger quoted companies are loaded with debt. They are fully laden and therefore sitting low in the water. The problem isn't just that institutional portfolios may be full of heavily laden larger corporations, but most particularly that they don't appear to have enough lifeboats!

Winning an analytical edge

The greatest amount of analytical brainpower in the financial industry is expended on the very largest companies. From an institutional point of view, getting a really big stock right will have a much more profound effect on the overall returns of a portfolio than a small one. Even the shrewdest call on a genuinely small company, however vibrant that tiny ant might be, cannot but pale in comparison. This line of thinking extends from the top of the market to the bottom.

The operations of larger companies are dissected and mulled over by battalions of analysts. Perversely this can work against the independence of the largest firms' management teams. Those that fail to follow conventional paths sometimes find themselves goaded into line by legions of market analysts and fund managers. This is one way that convergence has been forced upon the largest businesses.

And for investors, it's bad news for another reason. As a general rule, the tinier the stock, the greater the scope for its share price to be inefficient – and the more inaccurate the share price, the greater the opportunity for new shareholders to invest at a discounted valuation. The valuation inefficiency tends to be inversely proportionate to the market capitalisation of the company – so *the smaller the stock, the greater the analytical advantage*.

This is illustrated quite clearly within the smaller company universe. The bulk of analytical effort is poured into the slightly larger players while the genuinely small stocks in the FTSE SmallCap index have much less scrutiny. And those that are too small to feature in the FTSE SmallCap index, largely companies valued at under £50m, often have almost no independent research coverage at all.

Searching for
opportunities

There's limited research published on many of the smallest listed companies

Source: Bloomberg, based on number of brokers providing research coverage per stock within the FTSE SmallCap index, May 2014

As many of the smallest companies are rarely the subjects of independent research, their share prices can be grossly inaccurate relative to their earnings potential for days, months or sometimes even years. And while the shares of larger companies trade minute by minute or even second by second, smaller stocks might trade just a handful of times a day – or less.[35] Those investing in smaller companies not only have more chance of investing in a company that could buck the wider trend of economic stagnation, but also have greater chance of investing at a sub-normal valuation.

The key point is that there are advantages to smallness. These are more relevant at times when world growth is constrained, as it is now beyond the credit boom. And for those individuals looking for interesting prospects – rather fabulous investment peaches as I call them in my previous book – it's surely better to concentrate on fields that are a little less crowded than elsewhere.

Productivity differences

While some elements of smallness seem intuitive, it's more difficult to appreciate the linkages between productivity and smallness. However, there have been studies designed to capture the point at which the benefits of getting larger start to become outweighed by the problems that come with great size. One of the most detailed relates to an extraordinarily comprehensive study of more than 28,000 firms in Sweden's mining and manufacturing sector, drawing on ten years of data gathered by Swedish tax authorities running up to 2006.[36] This study, carried out by Professor Soderbom at the University of Gothenburg, suggests that, as companies grow, productivity can increase significantly in micro, small and medium-sized businesses due to economies of scale – but will become negative for operations with more than 250 staff.[37] The point at which efficiency starts to deteriorate appears to have a low threshold, but it's perhaps not too surprising to anyone working amidst the internecine problems of gigantic workforces.

---

35   On average, 30% of AIM stocks trade less than once a day. See Dimson, E. and Marsh, P. (2014), *Numis Smaller Companies Index Annual Review 2014* (Numis Securities), p.55.

36   Soderbom, M. and Sato, Y. (2011), 'Are larger firms more productive due to scale economies? A contrary evidence from Swedish microdata', seminar at University of Gothenburg.

37   Size definitions used here are not immediately transferable in terms of commonly used UK stock market definitions.

The benefits of diminutive scale for investors

So it seems that certain smaller companies can have some notable advantages over their larger competitors. But what is the scale of that advantage and how far do the advantages of smallness extend down the market capitalisation bands in the stock market? We can explore the power of smallness by comparing the historic performance of the wider market, which mainly encapsulates much larger businesses, with the returns achieved from investing in smaller listed companies. There's a long history of these kinds of studies.[38]

In nominal terms, equity markets have not done badly at all in the last 60 years or so. For example, investing just £1 in 1955 in the DMS All-Equity index[39] (the index that includes the majority of all UK-quoted companies, with weightings dominated by the largest of those companies) would have grown to £1,070 by the end of 2013.

This might seem quite substantial, but it includes income reinvested from dividend payments, which might have started at around 4% a year.[40] Over time, with economic growth and price inflation, those income payments have grown progressively – becoming much larger in comparison with the initial £1 invested. On top of that, if dividend income is reinvested, the return on the index includes the appreciation of the stock market *and* the appreciation on the reinvested income. So £1,070 might appear to be a very large return over that period; in annual terms, it's actually equivalent to a gain of just over 12% each year.

How does that compare with the long-run performance achieved by investing in genuinely small companies? In the UK, the longest data series benchmarking the performance of smaller companies is the Numis Smaller Companies Index (NSCI). It's made up of the smallest 10% of companies quoted on the LSE by value.[41] It was first published by Professors Elroy Dimson and Paul Marsh of the London Business School at the end of 1987, and index data has been updated every day since. The team has also taken historic data to replicate performance back to 1955. At the end of 2013, there were

---

38   Banz, R. (1981), 'The relationship between return and market value of common stocks', *Journal of Financial Economics*, 9, pp.3–18.

39   The DMS All-Equity index encompasses most UK-listed companies. As it is weighted by market capitalisation, its major weightings comprise the largest UK-quoted companies.

40   Dimson, E., Marsh, P. and Staunton, M. (2014), *Credit Suisse Global Investment Returns Sourcebook 2014* (Credit Suisse AG), pp.44.

41   Measured by market capitalisation.

some 352 companies tracked by the NSCI.[42] (The main NSCI excludes companies quoted on AIM, although there is a series that does include these stocks.)

Just £1 invested in the NSCI at the end of 1955 would have returned £4,907 by the end of 2013, far outstripping the £1,070 return achieved by the wider market. The annual percentage return from investing in the NSCI over that period would have been 15.5% – over 3% better than the market per annum[43] – a vast difference in investment terms. This trend is not unique to the UK; it has been observed in stock markets across the world.

But – pause for a moment here – the same £1 invested in the ultra-small world of the DMS MicroCap index[44] would have appreciated to £21,585! Note the giant differential in the performance of the very smallest listed companies. The tiniest have outperformed in an extraordinary way since 1955. The advantage of smaller companies is proportionate – the smaller the company, the better the performance on average. Hold onto this. It's important.

Of course, these figures are a little deceptive; they conceal the extent to which prices in the real world have also gone up over the years. There have been intermittent and sometimes substantial bursts of inflation. For example, prices rose by around 13% a year on average in the UK in 1970s. But if we adjust for that price effect,[45] the purchasing power of £1 invested in the NSCI with dividends reinvested would have increased 207 times over since 1955. And yes – with the same amount invested in the micro-cap index, purchasing power would of course be much greater still.[46]

42   Source: Numis Securities.

43   Dimson, E., Marsh, P. and Staunton, M. (2014), *Credit Suisse Global Investment Returns Sourcebook 2014* (Credit Suisse AG).

44   DMS MicroCap index: benchmark tracking the smallest 1% of UK-listed companies.

45   Using the RPI deflator; adjusted relative to changes in the cost of the goods referenced in the retail prices index.

46   Dimson, E. and Marsh, P. (2014), *Numis Smaller Companies Index Annual Review 2014* (Numis Securities).

The small company effect

Investing in the UK's smallest listed companies

£1

Investment

1955

DMS All-Equity Index

£1,070*

UK market

2013

Numis Smaller Companies Index

£4,907*

Small

DMS MicroCap Index

£21,585*

Micro

*Returns including capital gain with dividend income reinvested.
Source: Dimson, E. Marsh, P. and Staunton, M. (2002), *Triumph of the Optimists* (Princeton University Press), and subsequent research; Numis Smaller Companies Index
Cited in Dimson, E. Marsh, P. and Staunton, M. (2014), *Credit Suisse Global Investment Returns Sourcebook* (London Business School)

THE IMPORTANCE OF SCALE – INTRODUCING 'THE SMALL COMPANY EFFECT'

The moves of mainstream market indices are heavily determined by the share price moves of the largest companies. So for a long time most investors didn't quite know whether smallest companies really outperformed, or indeed whether such a trend was persistent over the long term.

The first academic study that rigorously compared stock market returns of groups of smaller quoted companies with larger ones was only published just over 30 years ago. In the case of the US, it seemed that smaller companies had indeed significantly outperformed their larger comparators, and that this trend was persistent over the longer term. Further studies have come to the same conclusion regarding performance in most other stock markets around the globe. An update in 2014 noted that since the year 2000, the investment returns from smaller companies outstripped larger ones in 21 of 23 economies worldwide.[47] Indeed academic studies are so consistent regarding the outperformance of smallness that the trend now has a name – it is known as **the small company effect**.

In the UK there is sufficient stock market data to test these performance differentials from 1955. The studies confirm that the small company effect is evident within the UK, and importantly that it is also proportionate to the size of the quoted companies. In other words, the smaller the quoted company, generally the better its performance. Of course, the trend does appear to fade or disappear at times – as it did in the UK during parts of the expansionary phase of the credit

---

47   Dimson, E., Marsh, P. and Staunton, M. (2014), *Credit Suisse Global Investment Returns Sourcebook 2014* (Credit Suisse AG). Small firm premium in 23 countries, period ending 31 December 2013. Chart 19, p.45.

boom. But over the long term, the returns on the very smallest quoted companies have in the past been notably better than other size bands of quoted stocks.

Sometimes the extraordinary magnitude of the difference between the largest and smallest quoted companies can be difficult to fully comprehend. In the UK, Royal Dutch Shell has a market value of around £152bn,[48] whereas some of the genuinely small quoted companies have market capitalisations of only £10m or even less. If the market capitalisation of Shell is equated with the height of Mount Everest, then a company valued at £10m wouldn't even reach one metre! Seen in this light it's hardly surprising that big and small companies have such different investment characteristics.

Finally it is worth highlighting that the stock prices of smaller companies can at times be more volatile than larger ones – that's not of great concern for longer-term investors but might be important to remember if you are investing on a relatively short-term time horizon.

It wouldn't be fair, of course, not to take the risks and higher costs of investing in smaller companies into consideration in these comparisons. Some investors are wary of investing in smaller companies because there may be fewer shares to buy and sell and because trading volumes might be low. In other words, the shares might be difficult to sell when markets turn. The extreme volatility of all sorts of share prices during the financial crisis in 2008 informs this view somewhat.[49]

But it's not the full story. Recently there has been significant research into liquidity and what it might mean for the overall returns made by investors. Intriguingly, it suggests that because the largest investors actively prefer investing in more liquid stocks, there

---

48   Source: Royal Dutch Shell, as at June 2014; includes both A and B shares.
49   Dimson, E. and Marsh, P. (2014), *Numis Smaller Companies Index Annual Review 2014* (Numis Securities), p.68.

might be a performance advantage to be had from investing in *less* liquid ones. And that advantage could increase the smaller the company becomes.

This has been studied by academics too. US stock market data was gathered between 1971 and 2012 and divided into four groups according to company size.[50] The stocks were then ranked according to the volume of trade in their shares, with the returns generated by the most actively traded 25% of stocks compared with the returns generated by the least actively traded quartile. The results showed that lesser traded stocks tended to outperform in all cohorts. And the performance differentials – shown in the illustration on the next page – were simply vast. Strangely enough, the more liquid micro-cap stocks performed the worst. Not just worse than the least liquid micro caps, but worse than all other cohorts too. The differential between the performance of the most liquid and the least liquid micro-cap stocks was over 14% on average each year.[51]

Once again, it is worth pausing for a moment here too. In this case, the most liquid quartile of micro-cap stocks underperformed dramatically, so it means that the stocks in the remaining three quartiles of micro caps must on average have outperformed by a greater margin, as otherwise the micro-cap universe wouldn't generate returns that exceed other areas of the market. Therefore, as long as the most liquid quartile of micro-cap stocks is avoided, the upside potential of the other micro-cap stocks is probably even greater than the average.

Finally, it is worth noting that the liquidity effect is evident even in stocks that are generally regarded as easily tradeable. Amongst the largest 25% of the large cap companies surveyed, the margin of difference between the returns on the least liquid and the most liquid stocks is over 2.5% per annum – a truly startling figure given that even the less-liquid large cap companies are generally traded regularly each day.[52]

---

50   As measured by market capitalisation.

51   Note that the geometric mean was used to compare properties with different value ranges, rather than the arithmetic mean. Calculations by R.G. Ibbotson et al., are detailed in footnote 55 of their paper.

52   Ibbotson, R.G., Chen, Z., Kim, D.Y-J., Hu, W.Y. (2013), 'Liquidity as an Investment Style', *Financial Analysts Journal*, vol. 69, no. 3. Updated 2014.

Size and liquidity

US quartile portfolio returns 1972–2013*

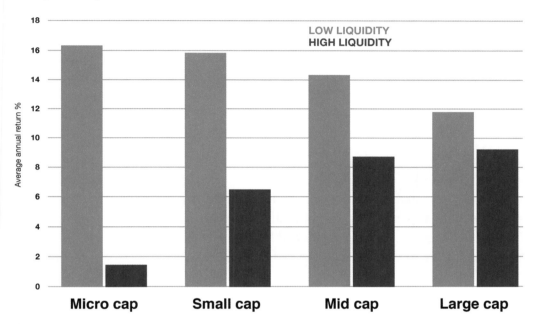

LOW LIQUIDITY
HIGH LIQUIDITY

Average annual return % — vertical axis: 0, 2, 4, 6, 8, 10, 12, 14, 16, 18

Micro cap   Small cap   Mid cap   Large cap

*Geometric mean

Source: Ibbotson, R.G., Chen, Z., Kim, D.Y-J.,Hu, W.Y. (2013), 'Liquidity as an Investment Style', *Financial Analysts Journal*, vol. 69, no. 3, updated 2014

A quick look back at 'The small company effect' illustration a couple of pages ago shows a similar trend whereby the smaller companies in the NSCI have outperformed the wider market over the last 58 years. It would be useful if the illiquidity and smaller companies strategies were entirely independent of each other as then their impacts could be potentially cumulative. However, we need to recognise that the two trends probably overlap; there may be a degree of double-counting. The good news is that the academic evidence all seems to point in the same direction.

It seems incontrovertible that there is real advantage to be had from including the smallest companies within portfolios. Generally the smaller the company, the better the potential return. Equally, the lower a stock's market liquidity, the better its potential return too. Whilst there may be higher transaction costs in the smaller stocks, these are relatively trivial relative to the higher returns. Lastly, in addition to offering scope for higher returns, the smaller company universe of investments offers diversification benefits too. The ecosystem of smaller companies has aspects that give it greater resilience, and investors in genuinely small stocks can prioritise these features.

The problem for institutions is that they have grown dependent on plentiful market liquidity during the boom – they like the flexibility of changing their minds on stocks or markets almost instantaneously at will. But this positioning is at odds with academic research, which suggests that the best performance might be found amongst the most illiquid stocks. (Remember that institutions have withdrawn almost all of their capital from genuinely small quoted companies during the recent credit boom and it will be difficult to reverse that trend given their lack of liquidity.)

Although the stock market research into the liquidity effect is relatively recent, there is a long history of monitoring performance and smallness. The conclusions of these studies are not 'one-off' findings. They are not strange anomalies that have been pinpointed once or twice and then could not be replicated. In fact, similar trends have been observed in many stock markets around the world, including in the US.[53]

---

53   Dimson, E., Marsh, P. and Staunton, M. (2014), *Credit Suisse Global Investment Returns Sourcebook 2014* (Credit Suisse AG).

The small company effect *

Investing in the US's smallest listed companies

$48,090 *

$29,400 *

$3,919 *

$1

Investment	Large	Small	Micro

1955 2013

*Returns including capital gain with dividend income reinvested.
Source: Dimson, E. Marsh, P. and Staunton, M. (2002), *Triumph of the Optimists* (Princeton University Press), and subsequent research; Numis Smaller Companies Index
Cited in Dimson, E., Marsh, P. and Staunton, M. (2014), *Credit Suisse Global Investment Returns Sourcebook* (London Business School)

The figures above conceal the fact that there have been extended periods when smaller companies have underperformed their larger contemporaries, most particularly over recent decades during the credit boom.[54] But, overall, the scale effect is so well-established that academics at the London Business School describe the size phenomenon as one of "the longest established and best-documented regularities" of the stock market.[55] Not exceptional at all – a regularity.

Conclusion

The growth potential of a smaller company tends to be more closely linked with factors specific to the individual company, rather than general economic trends. Some grow progressively even at times of recession, whilst others fail to do well even during a boom.

During times of plenty, both large and small companies tend to expand, so the differences in their growth potential are not especially striking. But when economic growth is sluggish, those with major market positions tend to struggle to achieve growth. In contrast, there is always a proportion of smaller companies with smaller market positions that finds ways to sustain momentum – even at difficult times. This difference in growth potential is widely observed across the world and is known as the small company effect.

The fact that smaller companies have better growth potential explains why they have significantly outperformed larger quoted companies over the years. In the 58 years to 2013, £1 invested in the smaller companies universe (as defined by the NSCI) delivered a return of £4,907, whereas the broad market, dominated by the larger companies, only delivered £1,070. Importantly, the small company effect is also proportionate. So investing in the very smallest quoted companies (in the universe defined by the DMS MicroCap index, for example) has delivered an even better return. Over the same 58 years to 2013, just £1 invested in the very smallest quoted companies delivered a simply enormous £21,585!

---

54   Detailed research into how far returns from UK smaller companies have deviated since 1955 shows the degree of dispersion and how the years of positive returns outweigh the negatives. See Dimson, E. and Marsh, P. (2014), 'Longer-Term Performance', *Numis Smaller Companies Index Annual Review 2014* (Numis Securities), p.59.

55   Dimson, E., Marsh, P. and Staunton, S. (2013), *Credit Suisse Global Investment Returns Sourcebook 2013* (Credit Suisse AG).

The problem for institutions is that they have grown dependent on plentiful market liquidity during the boom – they like the flexibility of changing their minds on stocks or markets almost instantaneously. But this positioning is at odds with academic research, which suggests that best performance is found amongst the most illiquid stocks. As institutions have progressively withdrawn almost all of their capital from genuinely small quoted companies in the last 25 years, this trend will be difficult to reverse.

Now that world growth has slowed beyond the boom, the differences in the investment characteristics of smaller companies are becoming highly relevant. The extra growth potential of smaller companies as well as their diversification benefits will become hugely desirable to institutions. UK portfolios containing both large and smaller companies are likely to deliver better and more sustainable returns, and there are literally hundreds and hundreds of smaller companies listed in the UK that together form a wide-ranging and diverse ecosystem.

What are the characteristics that might help identify the most promising smaller companies from an investment perspective? And in particular, what other characteristics combine well with general smallness to deliver enhanced returns? These are the questions that the next chapter will address.

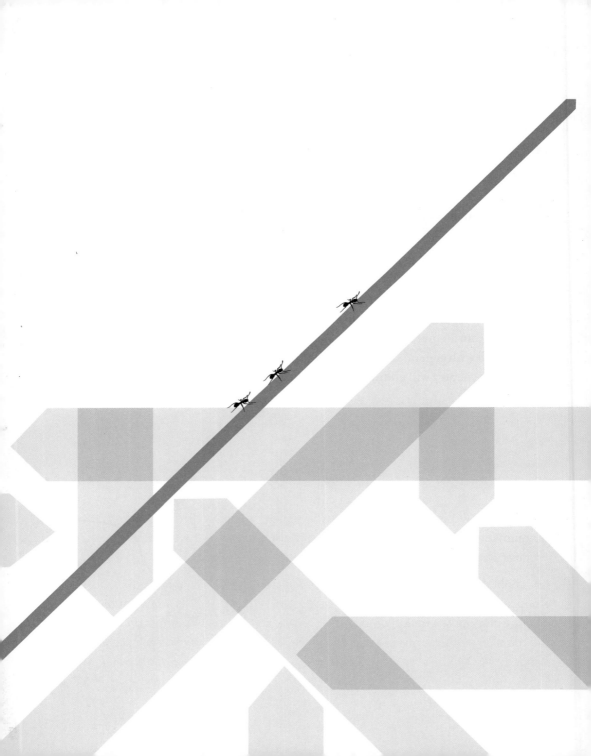

CHAPTER 4

Exploring Value, Growth and

ss

and share prices

...icipating in growth, it would seem logical to expect those
...rospects to deliver the best returns. This thesis appears so
...al to expect anything else. Indeed, a quick glance at the
...s operating in the UK smaller companies arena reinforces
...d funds focusing on smaller quoted companies state that
their primary aim is to invest in businesses with above-average growth so that they deliver
premium returns.[56] And yet there are troubling aspects about growth stocks – stocks whose
earnings are expected to increase faster than the market average.

You might remember the excitement of the dotcom era, when companies like the software
producer Autonomy plc were listed in the UK.[57] Following its initial public offering
(IPO), Autonomy's exciting potential for above-average growth drove up its share price
and the stock outperformed. So far, so good. Indeed, Autonomy was an excellent growth
company – well above average. Despite subsequent setbacks for most dotcom stocks,

---

56   Factsheets profiled by *FE Trustnet*, June 2014.

57   Autonomy's UK listing took place in 2000. It was listed prior to this on NASDAQ in the US and EASDAQ in Europe.

Autonomy went on to deliver growth for another 11 years, and even benefited from a takeover bid for the company at the end of that period.

Yet its share price fell in absolute terms and actually **underperformed** the wider market between its London IPO in 2000 and its takeover by Hewlett-Packard in 2011. Have a look at the share price chart:

Autonomy
Share price 2000–2011

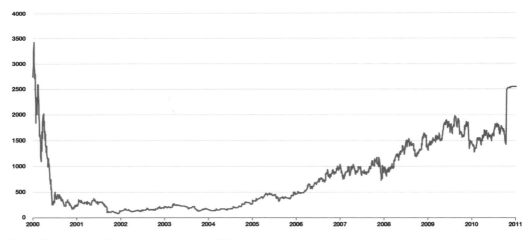

Source: Historic data supplied by Thomson Reuters, June 2014

With the benefit of hindsight, we can see that within a few months of issue, Autonomy's share price had already peaked. Although it continued to be successful as a business, investor expectations had become so high that even sustained growth over the following years could not drive the stock price back above its previous heady levels.

Autonomy may be an extreme case, but in general share prices of growth stocks tend to rise much too far, too fast.[58] The momentum of the crowd pushes valuations higher

---

58   Fama, E. and French, F. (1998), 'Value versus Growth: The International Evidence', *Journal of Finance*, 53 (6), 1975–1999.

than the ability of growth stocks to deliver. In these situations, human emotion is in the driving seat. We all like discussing an exciting investment case, and as buyers cluster around an exciting story, the valuations of the stocks in question inevitably move up further than they should on strictly rational grounds.

Because of this, investment strategies specifically designed to select companies that are forecast to deliver above-average growth tend to carry within themselves the seeds of their own downfall. Strategies that are skewed towards selecting stocks from a universe of growth companies leave the investor little or no margin for error. Even if a company succeeds in growing earnings at an exceptional pace, the overall investment return can still be disappointing, because share prices tend to run ahead of the ability of companies to deliver.

There's another problem too. When expectations are high, it's tough to exceed them. So high-expectation stocks tend to fall back badly if the underlying business slows or stops growing. In 2000, most dotcom stocks didn't get anywhere near to meeting market expectations for their growth, and their share prices went into free-fall.

The risk/reward ratio for growth stocks is stacked against the investor. Well-known stocks like Apple and Microsoft may have outperformed at times, but far too often growth investors end up making sub-normal returns because expectations become over-inflated.

Introducing income and value stocks

We know that growth stocks can underperform, so perhaps investors should be asking different questions and taking a different approach. Why not focus on recovery stocks instead? Look back at the Autonomy chart on the previous page. Those who bought the stock in 2002 or 2004 went on to make attractive returns. So a good starting point may be to look for those stocks where investors have *already* been disappointed and expectations are rock bottom. Logic suggests that their valuations might have fallen too far as emotional investors sought to sell their holdings at almost any price.

The good news for incoming investors is that in some instances the dividend yield of such companies can be a lot higher than most other stocks. It may be that some of these stocks may not be expected to grow much, but a high dividend yield can be more important for income investors.

In the case of non-dividend payers, some have fallen so far in value that the value of their tangible assets or indeed the scale of the cash flow generated by the business exceeds the value of the company itself. Companies meeting these criteria are known as value investments.

Interestingly, academic evidence suggests that both income and value investments routinely outperform go-go growth companies. Indeed, income and value stocks tend to outperform wider stock market indices too. There is a subtle reason for this. Growth stocks often attract new investors when they are close to new peaks, as the momentum of an exciting story draws in more investors. Such companies need to continue to meet and beat demanding market expectations in order to sustain a premium rating on the stock. Over time, this becomes harder and harder to achieve. Eventually growth stocks must inevitably fail to sustain rapid growth. Their share prices then revert to the mean and fall back.

In contrast, a recent disappointment or absence of growth is the dominant factor for both income and value investments. Normally new investors are buying such companies at depressed valuations. For the buyer, this tends to feel uncomfortable, as stock prices might continue to fall in the face of further bad news. Even those stocks that don't decline often fail to grow for years, thereby missing out on any general rise of the market.

But the good news is that most market participants don't expect income or value investments to generate decent growth anyway. And, should they do so, their valuations revert to the mean – which is normally considerably higher than the level at which they have been trading. Sometimes the trigger is a result of a change in the management team, or it might be related to a change in an industry trend or a takeover. Occasionally even bad news can be met with an increase in the share price, if the deterioration is less severe than had been expected. The key point is that low expectations are endemic in both income and value investments. That means that if the scenario turns out to better than expected – even just a little better – then they can outperform handsomely.

In the meantime, as long as those with a premium yield continue to sustain their dividends, income investors receive extra return on their investments that may, in part, offset the lack of growth. Meanwhile value stocks, in particular, are prone to takeovers, as others seek to acquire undervalued assets or cash flow generated by the business.

So when it comes to choosing the best investment strategy, chasing those companies forecast to grow at the fastest rate won't necessarily deliver the best returns. Growth investments that grow a little slower than expected can be outperformed by moribund income or value businesses that have experienced quite modest growth, albeit at a level that is greater than anticipated. On the stock market, these features have been evident for decades and decades. Clearly there are periods when the long-term trend reverses. Stocks with growth characteristics have periods of outperformance. But in time this fades and income and value stocks catch up and outperform to a greater degree.

Combining smallness, value and income

The previous chapter outlined how the NSCI has outperformed the wider market since 1955. This is the small company effect in action. If, like smallness, investment strategies that focus on value and income stocks also outperform, then it's worth investigating to what degree these factors might have combined in the past to deliver extra returns. How effective might they be together?

Professors Elroy Dimson and Paul Marsh, along with Mike Staunton, a more-recent arrival on the team, have used the NSCI database to tease out an answer to this question. Initially they subdivided the universe of smaller companies defined by the NSCI by market capitalisation. The largest 30% were classified as 'relatively large', with the rest defined as 'relatively small'. They also categorised the stocks in the index as either value or growth. They defined value companies as those with a high book-to-market (BTM) ratio,[59] calculated by taking the value of tangible assets and dividing it by the market capitalisation of the company. Those companies with lots of assets such as cash, property or finished stock can be regarded as being at the value end of the spectrum. In contrast, those with a relatively large stock market valuation relative to their tangible assets must have other factors driving the share price. These are grouped together as growth stocks.

After this exercise, the professors had four groups of companies. Based on their characteristics, they labelled them as 'Big Growth', 'Big Value', 'Small Growth' and 'Small Value'.[60] (Remember that all the companies with the 'big' label were part of the NSCI, so they were only big on a relative basis. All the companies in this analysis ranked amongst the smallest 10% of stocks on the LSE.)

The performance of these different groups was recorded each year, with contributions of each stock weighted by scale (measured by stock market capitalisation). So a relatively large stock that outperformed would have a greater weighting in the overall group return than one of the smallest stocks that outperformed by a similar amount. At the end of each year, the stocks were reclassified once again, so that if the share price of a growth stock fell back sharply for some reason it might be reclassified a value stock for the subsequent year.

The results of this analysis are very revealing.

---

59   As used by Eugene Fama and Kenneth French.
60   Excepting the middle 20% of companies measured by BTM, which were excluded.

NSCI 1955–2013
excludes investment companies

£1

Investment

1955

£1,795*

Small growth

£2,631*

Big growth

£24,915*

Big value

£61,233*

Small value

2013

*Returns including capital gain with dividend income reinvested.
Source: Dimson, E. and Marsh, P. (2014), *Numis Smaller Companies Annual Review*

The tearaway leader in terms of performance was the group of 'Small Value' stocks – outperforming by quite some distance. On average, these stocks delivered more than seven percentage points more than 'Big Growth' stocks each year. That means that investing in growth stocks at the bigger end of the NSCI would have turned £1 into just over £2,600 over 58 years; but investing in smaller stocks with value characteristics over the same period would have turned it into over £61,000.

We know that value stocks tend to outperform amongst FTSE 100 and FTSE 250 stocks, but the value effect is hugely more effective in the smaller company universe. The bottom line of this analysis is surely that **size really matters.**

Better still, even after taking inflation into account, the small value strategy returned on average more than 15% each year. These are real returns on an extraordinary scale.

Value and smallness beyond the credit boom

As companies grow, they tend to raise finance in one of two forms. They borrow money from others, which they have to repay in the future. Or they raise risk capital, offering investors a share of the company in exchange for cash – a share which may ultimately be worth a lot more than the sum invested if the company is successful.

The great advantage of raising risk capital is that there's *no* obligation for the company to pay interest or dividends to the holders of the shares. The disadvantage is that issuing equity dilutes the ownership of the business for those who already own stock.

Quoted companies usually use a mix of debt and risk capital to fund their growth. The proportion of each is a matter of judgment. Those companies with no debt tend to have greater resilience and flexibility because they have no obligation to pay out interest or find cash to repay borrowing at specific dates in the future.

As outlined in Chapter 2, it was advantageous for businesses to take on more debt during the credit boom. Gearing up with extra debt meant the possibility of participating in the boom in greater scale at a time when asset prices were rising. In addition, interest rates were trending downwards, so those with debt enjoyed falling interest costs too. It was also relatively easy to refinance debt upon the relevant repayment date with yet more debt, simply extending its duration.

During the boom, shareholders tended to get better returns in companies that used extra debt to finance growth. But this strategy carries extra risk. At times of major economic setback, most businesses are vulnerable and profits decline. At these points, the need to sustain interest payments irrespective of underlying profitability can be unwelcome. The situation can be particularly problematic for those who need to refinance, particularly if banks are less profitable and pulling back as well.

Many companies were caught out by these problems in 2008. Most indebted companies were bailed out to some degree by the emergency reduction in UK interest rates to just 0.5% in 2009. Many breached the terms of their loan agreements and some were forced to raise new capital. If profitability is declining, it can be difficult to get access to finance, and so many companies issued extra shares at a point when their share prices were already depressed. It was highly dilutive to existing shareholders. Those who failed to raise enough capital went bust; their shareholders lost everything.

This highlights exactly why investors need to keep right up to date on the mix of risk capital and debt within a business. However attractive its long-term prospects, a company with an unsafe debt burden carries a sizeable risk that the equity return is either heavily diluted by the issuance of further shares, perhaps at a distressed price, or that the company is forced into liquidation and equity holders lose their *entire* investment.

When I have lost out as an investor, I have lost out fastest and most completely on businesses with overextended balance sheets. The scale of their debt simply became too large in comparison with their risk capital. Investors need to understand that some stocks that have fallen out of favour and tick the value box sometimes have overextended balance sheets too. Indeed, some smaller companies may well be overextended. Some of these companies used to be large, but their stock price collapsed in 2008 and in 2014 they are still trying to address their lack of risk capital. In my experience, it is worth avoiding this kind of small company, however alluring they may seem. Their shares can be very volatile.

But, reassuringly, there are value stocks to be found with relatively little debt within the business – or even surplus cash. Over the course of the credit boom, as discussed, many banks concentrated their lending on larger borrowers, where they could lend in industrial quantities. By scaling back on their smaller company lending, they have inadvertently helped ensure there is an unusually large group of companies out there with both the advantage of smallness *and* strong balance sheets. This balance sheet strength of many ant-sized stocks is a commercial advantage that is very much under-appreciated.

Conclusion

It's easy to see why most investors prioritise growth when selecting their investments. But unfortunately many get a little overenthusiastic about the companies with the highest growth potential. Frequently their share prices rise to over-anticipate that growth, and in due course any signs that those companies might fail to deliver on those elevated expectations can result in disappointment and falling share prices.

In contrast, stocks that have not grown much – most particularly companies that have disappointed investors in the past – tend to attract rather less excitement. These are often classified as income or value stocks. The lack of excitement that surrounds them means that these stocks often stand at valuations that over-discount their negatives. In time, the share prices of those that do find ways to slightly improve their prospects tend to outperform.

The small company effect can be enhanced through combining it with other market trends that also tend to generate premium returns. Specifically, in the past, the investment returns achieved by pursuing both 'smallness' and 'value' amongst the tiniest of listed companies have been quite extraordinary.

Given that the smaller company universe underperformed for large parts of the credit boom, there are good reasons to anticipate that there might be plenty of value stocks to be found. The fact that many banks have scaled back their lending to smaller companies means that there is also a disproportionate number of stocks with strong balance sheets as well as value characteristics. So overall it seems that genuinely small companies are unusually well-placed to outperform over the coming years. In particular, that outperformance could be most exceptional amongst the tiniest ant-sized companies, particularly those with above-average assets on their balance sheets.

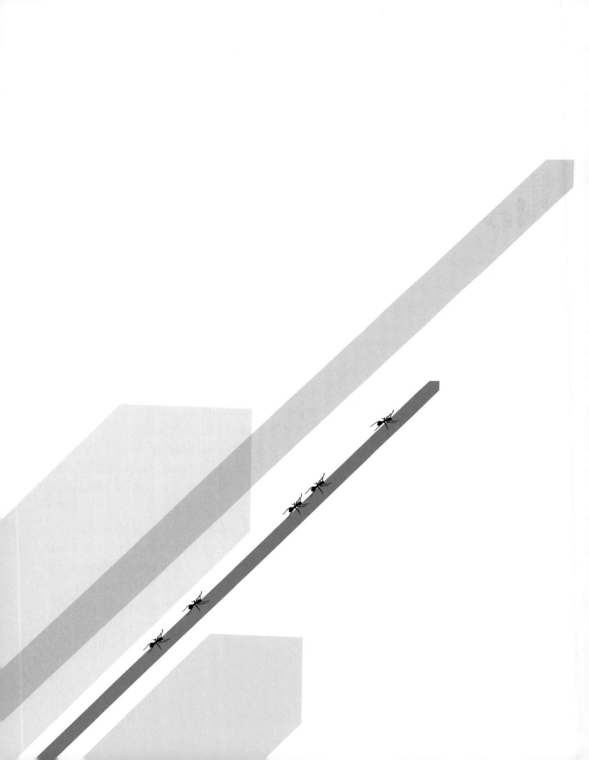

CHAPTER 5

How AIM is Aligned with Smallness

Stock picking for the best returns

Each year the list of the UK's top stock market performers invariably includes a cluster of small and micro-cap stocks. In 2013, a handful of AIM-quoted stocks rose more than 100%.[61] Generally 2013 may have been a good year for smaller companies, but it's not uncommon for quite a number to rise by more than 50% most years. Occasionally some larger companies appear amongst the list, but more often than not, they tend to be mainly or exclusively small. Even during the decades when smaller companies have lagged, there are always a large number of small companies that have delivered double digit percentage returns.

As post credit boom trends start to assert themselves, genuinely small stocks delivering these kinds of returns will become more important to investors. But for a really successful investment, it's not just about trying to get lucky over a single year. It's about spotting the potential to make an attractive return over time, perhaps over years and years. So how can an investor determine which stocks have the best upside over the longer term?

---

61   Harrington, J. (2013), 'A good year to take AIM', *Proactive Investors*, 2 January 2014.

With this question in mind, a favourite example of mine is Bloomsbury Publishing.[62] Founded in the late 1980s, the company's flotation in 1994 raised £5.5m which it used to develop its paperback arm and children's lists.[63] It has grown significantly over the years, principally through organic growth, but supplemented by acquisition too. One of the advantages of being a very small company that is listed is that the business can grow at a faster rate if shareholders fund additional investment through buying extra shares. Clearly one reason for Bloomsbury's growth was its skill in publishing the first Harry Potter book in 1997, and developing that into a massive success with the six subsequent titles in the same series.

One of the key contributors to that success was the fact that Bloomsbury backed the first Harry Potter book with substantial investment to bring it to everyone's attention. Although Bloomsbury was tiny relative to the publishing majors, the management team had the risk capital available that meant it could compete with those larger rivals in their investment in marketing. The cost of the extra marketing did not force Bloomsbury to take on additional debt which might have become a burden if the Harry Potter series had failed to take off. Bloomsbury had extra risk capital, and so it had the scope to back several other potential winners with all of the upside potential, yet without the downside risk of saddling the company with potentially excessive debts.

In the late 90s, the risk/reward ratio for investors was highly attractive, given that the scale of the upside more than outweighed the modest downside risk. However, being small, the spin-off benefits of Harry Potter's subsequent success were also disproportionately large for Bloomsbury in other ways too. Once the appeal of the books became apparent, Bloomsbury was able to use its success to forge new relationships with some of the biggest and best authors around the world. It was then able to take advantage of this established network to distribute its other publications.

Bloomsbury used the momentum of its early success to generate additional capital and invest that in further growth. Amazingly, even after 20 years of premium growth, Bloomsbury has still not yet grown big enough to be a mid-cap stock. It's still a publisher with scope to expand.

---

62   Funds administered by Miton Group plc are invested in Bloomsbury Publishing plc as at June 2014.

63   Source: Bloomsbury plc, June 2014.

Companies like Bloomsbury are not only attractive investments because they outperform, but also because they can build an increasingly valuable market position over the years. Bloomsbury's share price has reflected the ups and downs of the stock market along the way, but the volatility has been moderated by the progressive increase of its dividend. The returns on these kinds of stocks are the antithesis of those favoured during the credit boom, because the investment return is not reliant on skillful buying and selling. Shareholders who bought the stock at the time of float have benefited from a share price that has gone up over five-fold, and if the dividends were reinvested in buying more shares along the way then the return is rather more than nine-fold. One of the reasons that smaller companies like Bloomsbury can deliver attractive returns is because their advantages are sustainable for a considerable time. It is precisely their immaturity and smallness at the time of their flotation that means they have scope to succeed for years and years, without becoming so large that they dominate their markets.

Competing with the professionals

So more durable investment returns are made on companies that grow progressively over time – regular businesses like Bloomsbury. Naturally there will be some competition to identify such investments before they become obviously successful – but not necessarily as much as might be assumed from professional fund managers. Whilst smallcap fund managers certainly prize investments like Bloomsbury, they are rather more constrained in their stock selection than most appreciate. Most don't have unfettered freedom to select the most attractive stocks across the full universe of smaller companies.

During the boom, most institutions have skewed the focus of their analysis towards the most liquid companies. The ability to buy and sell shareholdings relatively quickly is perceived as important and this attitude has become so ingrained that most institutions rule out researching the most illiquid stocks. This is a costly luxury given the data in the 'Size and liquidity' illustration in Chapter 3. In *every* size band, from large to micro, the less liquid stocks delivered far greater investment returns than the more liquid ones.[64] However, in the eyes of most institutions, smallness is equated with illiquidity, so the smallest stocks are generally avoided. Perhaps this stance is rational to some degree. If you take another look at that illustration, you can see that if liquid stocks are a necessity,

---

64   US study running from 1972–2011. Cited in Ibbotson, R.G., Chen, Z., Kim, D.Y-J., Hu, W.Y. (2013), 'Liquidity as an Investment Style', *Financial Analysts Journal*, vol. 69, No. 3: 30–44. Updated 2014.

then it makes absolute sense to rule out investment in micro caps. The returns on the most liquid micro caps were almost zero in the US between 1971 and 2011.

Institutions often formalise their approach to illiquidity through imposing an arbitrary size limit below which they won't invest, irrespective of the attractiveness of the investment case. Limits that have been in place for many years will slow up the ability of institutions to flex as change comes through – even in the face of new trends that are obvious and progressive. The problem is that a major change of orientation is required, and mental taboos are difficult to discard. Only after the new trends have been in place for many years will institutions start to accept that the status quo needs to change. Ultimately they will need to take a little more liquidity risk to deliver better returns for their clients in a more sustainable way.

For now, institutions still equate their commercial interests with outperforming the market average for their clients. To some degree, they outsource the range of potential portfolio holdings to those that compile the benchmarks. The most established index representing UK quoted smaller companies is the NSCI, which in its standard form only includes companies listed on the LSE. Many smallcap funds use it as their yardstick. However, over the last two decades many of the smallest LSE-quoted stocks have relisted on the AIM exchange. And smaller companies' flotations tend to come to AIM rather than the LSE too, so a vast number of the smallest companies are now excluded from the standard NSCI. These factors have greatly changed the investment characteristics of this benchmark universe over recent decades. LSE-listed companies with market capitalisations up to £1,500m now fall into the NSCI definition of smaller companies, whereas in 1988 the largest index member was only valued at just over £100m![65] Those funds with the NSCI as a benchmark have gradually migrated away from genuinely smaller companies that are well-set to deliver outperformance in the future.

There are some other smallcap funds that use the FTSE SmallCap index as their benchmark. This index only includes LSE-listed stocks too, and therefore also excludes all the smaller companies listed on the AIM exchange. In 2014, the largest stock within the FTSE SmallCap index (excluding investment companies) was valued at close to £600m; its smallest was worth around £50m.[66] So although this universe of smaller companies doesn't include larger companies that are part of the NSCI, it unfortunately

65   Dimson, E. and Marsh, P. (2014), *Numis Smaller Companies Index 2014 Annual Review* (Numis Securities).

66   FTSE Group, as at September 2014.

excludes nearly all the smallest UK-listed companies, either because they are AIM-listed or because the few that are still listed on the LSE fall below the lower index boundary.

The big problem with most benchmarks is that the movements of the largest stocks in the index have a disproportionate effect on overall index returns. This is a particular problem for the fund manager if one or two of these larger stocks outperform by a huge amount. With their larger weighting and their outperformance, the returns on a couple of stocks can skew the return of the entire index over a quarter or two. Therefore most professional fund managers are in a state of constant anxiety over missing out on the potential gains from the largest companies in the index. Institutions are really keen to ensure they don't underperform by a significant amount, so the fund managers feel they are obliged to participate in larger index stocks that appear likely to outperform in the short term – almost irrespective of the investment risks. Sometimes it is the most speculative companies, with unstable burdens of debt, which do get lucky in the short term and run ahead.

Therefore most smallcap fund managers spend a disproportionate amount of their time studying the largest stocks in their benchmark, which dilutes the time they can focus on the tinier stocks that might have a better chance of outperforming over the long term. Missing out on the outperformance of a tiny stock is not terrifying for an institution; it tends to have such a small impact on overall returns. But missing out on the lightning run of one of the largest constituents, irrespective of the fact that it may have little chance of sustainable success, gets plenty of attention – even when it involves backing a speculative business with an unstable balance sheet. This is known as benchmark tyranny. It skews the attention of institutional investors away from the potential winners amongst genuinely small quoted companies.

Clearly many professional fund managers recognise that some genuinely small companies that float might have attractive risk/reward ratios in the same way that Bloomsbury did. Most smaller company specialists do invest some capital in AIM-quoted stocks too. But generally both of these kinds of stocks are regarded as outside the benchmark, and therefore excluded from portfolios unless they have a much better risk/reward ratio than an equivalent stock within the relevant benchmark universe. Most smallcap fund managers do prefer stocks with strong balance sheets too, but frequently they have to overlook this preference if a large index weighting looks as if it could catch them out. Those with the NSCI benchmark are generally obliged to stock-pick mainly from within an investment universe that is dominated by mid caps, and also well picked over by larger stock managers. Indeed, the intensity of attention in this area of the market has forced valuations up to ratings that are significantly above most smallcaps and most of the stocks in the FTSE 100 too.

This mid-cap bias steers stock selectors into many companies that have used borrowing to enhance returns during the boom. It dilutes their interest in tiny companies that often have net cash balances and have underperformed over the last decade or two. It often leads them away from stocks that have lots of assets relative to their market capitalisation and away from stocks that are inefficiently priced due to an absence of research.

Of course, there are some smaller quoted companies with value or income characteristics and strong balance sheets within the NSCI. But there are much larger numbers of these kinds of stocks quoted on AIM. AIM-listed stocks appear to have much greater potential beyond the boom.

AIM: The leading exchange for smaller quoted stocks?

Let's not shirk the issue – many investors have not made decent returns on AIM-listed stocks. The exchange has experienced waves of IPO activity and often the returns delivered by the most fashionable sectors have not been as good as hoped. Nearly all the stocks listed at the time of the dotcom boom, for example, failed to go on to deliver attractive returns. Many of the mining or oil exploration stocks that listed on AIM over the last ten years have also fallen short of expectations.

Many of these are event-driven businesses with negative cash flow, looking to make a sizeable capital return when they strike it rich. However, with their adverse cash flow, their future funding is wholly dependent on the mood of the market; most rely on raising additional capital just to stay alive. These businesses are fundamentally unstable in that if they fail to raise capital over a fixed time period they are in danger of going bust – an outcome that can lead to shareholders losing their entire investment. Event-driven companies struggle to ride out periods where commodity prices or other asset prices are low. And irrespective of the fundamentals, if shareholders aren't inclined to support subsequent issues, the original investors tend to be heavily diluted by share issues at distressed prices. Dotcom and strike-it-rich stocks are credit boom stocks. They are often highly speculative, with most shareholders seeking to sell out for a quick capital profit on a favourable announcement.

But there are plenty of AIM-listed stocks that are well-placed to deliver premium returns with rather less excitement and investment risk. These are more conventional businesses with regular turnover and profits like Bloomsbury. These companies have the advantage of generating cash flow each year, which means these companies are relatively resilient and likely to endure. This contrasts with more speculative stocks, which are highly vulnerable because they burn through their cash and have a finite investment timetable.

Many regular stocks have delisted from the LSE and relisted on AIM to take advantage of the tax benefits and the less onerous costs of fundraising. Many of these stocks have not had a high profile during the credit boom on account of their diminutive scale, and because many haven't necessarily been growing especially rapidly. But as outlined in Chapter 3, during normal market conditions (i.e. outside of credit surges) it's the smallest listed companies that have delivered the best performance.

Crucially, there are not many exchanges in the world that include decent numbers of very small quoted companies. Despite the adverse trends during the credit boom, when many professional investors came to associate smallness with irrelevance, the UK government has helped the tiniest maintain a viable route to external capital through tax-based incentives. Venture capital trusts (VCTs)[67] and enterprise investment schemes (EIS)[68] have been put in place for this reason. These schemes work on an annual cycle, raising capital around each tax year-end, with the new capital held for up to two years until investments that meet the relevant criteria are identified. Many of these schemes have focused specifically on backing the smallest quoted stocks on AIM.

In my view, these schemes sustained AIM when it might otherwise have shrunk alarmingly; for example, after markets peaked in 2000 when the number of investors backing the smallest and most illiquid quoted companies declined significantly. The capital within the VCT and EIS schemes, raised during the good years, was essentially patient capital, invested progressively over time, and remaining invested for the long-term. So the AIM exchange remained open to fund the smallest quoted micro-cap fundraisings even when market conditions were unsettled.

---

67   VCT: A form of listed closed-end fund which invests in small unlisted firms, with the aim of generating high risk-adjusted returns. VCTs are compelled to invest a proportion of funds in companies with gross assets below a defined threshold and with a limit on total employee numbers.

68   EIS offer tax reliefs to investors in small and unquoted businesses. Stocks on AIM are regarded as unquoted in this context.

The fact that AIM has remained open to raising additional capital for some very small companies for most of the difficult years has meant that many other companies have chosen it for their IPO listing too. Meanwhile nearly all other exchanges focused on the smallest companies have shrunk alarmingly or ceased to exist at all – the AIM exchange has been most unusual in bucking the wider trend. As rival indices have disappeared, some smaller companies looking to retain their quoted status have relisted on AIM. The bottom-line is that AIM now stands among the most well-established and vibrant markets for small and micro-cap quoted stocks in the world. Its breadth and depth are remarkable.

The diversity of AIM

Taking AIM: A diverse universe of small companies
Distribution of companies by equity market value

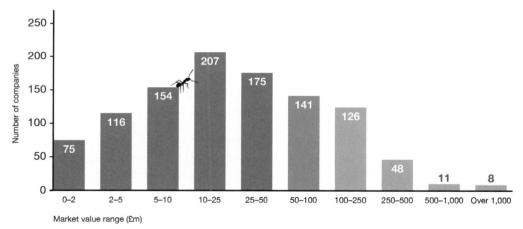

It may be that many of these stocks have not had a high profile on account of their diminutive scale; many have not attracted the excitement of speculative interest. But as outlined in Chapter 3, it's the smallest companies that have a history of delivering the best performance. AIM is nearly unique in having a rich universe of these kinds of stocks for investors to pick over.

Of course, not all regular businesses with regular customers, even those listed on AIM, have the potential to increase turnover, profit and cash flow in the future. But unlike more-speculative companies, steady cash-generative companies can deliver over an open-ended timeline. Businesses like the publisher Bloomsbury don't normally run out of cash, because they keep generating more each year. They have real staying power. These regular businesses can be investments for the long term, since the return is less dependent on buying or selling the shares at the right moment. There are lots of companies with good and growing cash flow on the AIM exchange. And it's interesting to note that most of the new flotations coming to AIM over recent years are those with similar characteristics. Few investors are chasing speculative companies any longer.

The AIM exchange is distinctive from other markets around the world because it has such a wide range of regular quoted businesses, and it has potential to list a whole lot more.

AIM and the forthcoming super-cycle in small cap returns

For many smaller quoted AIM stocks, the credit boom has been marked by a lack of institutional support and a refusal to even consider investing in companies below a particular size threshold. In fact, for much of the last two and a half decades, there have been many more institutions looking to sell rather than to buy small and micro-cap stocks, as attention shifted elsewhere.

From an investment perspective, artificial cut-offs which ignore companies below a minimum market capitalisation are demonstrably self-defeating. Applying such logic suggests that investors should avoid investing in a company standing on a PE[69] of 1×, with a 30% yield (if sustainable, a clearly undervalued firm) solely on account of its smallness. And yet the very same investors might recommend investing in the very same business at a share price that was ten times higher, just because its value moved above a specific market capitalisation threshold. Although the valuation still might have its attractions, with a PE of 10× and a yield of 3%, investors would have missed out on a tenfold increase in the value of the company.

---

69   PE: Price/earnings ratio: the ratio of a company's current share price to earnings per share.

During the credit boom, such thinking was tolerated because most mainstream equity indices delivered returns well above inflation. Now that world growth has moderated, and many larger businesses are struggling to deliver sustained growth, these investment opportunities will become rather more distinctive. Restrictions preventing an investment in companies below an arbitrary market capitalisation will become less tolerable, quite apart from the fact that such thinking has the intellectual stature of a paperclip!

Going forward, other factors will change too. It seems likely that speculative capital will not only be less successful but also less plentiful, and there will be greater focus on finding ways for portfolios to deliver attractive returns even when market indices are flat. This will force institutional investors to reallocate their capital into areas that can deliver in a slower growth environment. In time it will be recognised that the outperformance of companies like Bloomsbury rests on their ability to put new investment capital to really good use. Some big companies can invest sizeable amounts of investment capital to get a decent return. But the chances of success are so much greater amongst smaller companies that invest smaller sums and only need modest increments of market share to improve overall returns on their businesses.

However, the real upside for smaller companies comes with the availability of external capital. There will be some smaller private companies that take some modest risk to get a disproportionate return on their investments. But these opportunities will be so much more plentiful for quoted businesses, because their listing offers them access to extra capital. In contrast to the last couple of decades, once again it will be highly advantageous for genuinely small companies to have a market quote. In Bloomsbury's case, it was the combination of its ability to spot a winner, and the fact that it had good access to risk capital, that improved the risk/reward ratio so that its success could be so substantial.

During the boom years, the progressive withdrawal of institutional support for the smallest quoted companies led most regular smaller companies that lacked speculative appeal to stand on relatively low valuations. Investors often made much higher returns elsewhere through participating in the rise of various asset prices. However, as market trends change, something rather wonderful will happen. Some of the smallest companies with regular turnover, profits and cash flow will find that they are generating much greater investor interest – particularly if they are able to increase their productivity and generate extra cash returns. It will be easier to fund these investments at valuations that generate highly attractive risk/reward ratios. The more individual stocks outperform, the more those institutions that are underweight and underperforming will miss out. Ultimately, as institutional capital starts to flow back into smallness, valuations will be driven up further. All these factors will contribute to the outperformance of the AIM exchange. Not all the winners will be as good as Bloomsbury. But there will be more winners, and their returns will attract additional capital from other parts of the investment world.

One of the inherent characteristics of small and micro-cap stocks is their market illiquidity. Small and micro-cap stocks are by their very nature diminutive in scale and therefore have relatively modest turnover in their shares. Over the last two decades this has worked against them. Illiquid markets with excess sellers tend to overreact in terms of price movements, and this is one explanation as to why valuations on many smaller companies have sometimes fallen to extraordinarily low levels.

But illiquidity can work both ways. In the past institutions withdrew capital, and this depressed valuations, making it harder for companies to use external capital. Going forward, growing institutional interest in smallness will make it easier for smaller quoted companies to fund expansion at a more reasonable cost. There will never have been a better time to be a regular company with sustained turnover, profits and cash flow along with a listing. Indeed, all the evidence points to this being the start of a super-cycle for returns in the genuinely small – as last experienced between the mid-1950s and the mid-1980s.

AIM-listed companies
Reasons to be cheerful

Analytical advantage
The smaller the stock, the greater the advantage. There's more scope for valuations of small and micro-cap stocks to be incorrect and better opportunities to invest at discounted valuations.

Value stocks, particularly smaller ones, tend to outperform the most
There are plenty of AIM-quoted companies that fall into both small and value categories; that suggests scope to outperform over the coming years.

Balance sheet strength
The financial strength of many AIM stocks is underappreciated. At times of economic setback, companies with the strongest balance sheets can take the greatest advantage, especially quoted companies that can raise further capital when others are constrained.

Institutional capital meets AIM market illiquidity
As institutions allocate more capital to a market that's highly illiquid, the valuations of AIM-listed stocks might move to sizeable premiums in a process that could take several years.

Premium valuations on AIM stocks will accelerate their growth
As small/micro-cap stocks move to premium valuations, the earnings enhancement from their fundraisings will accelerate their potential in contrast to the more constrained growth of larger companies.

The advantages of smallness in a slower growth world
There are many advantages to smallness, but these are most relevant at times when world growth is subdued. The hangover from the credit boom can be countered by the advantages of small and micro-cap stocks, most particularly those quoted on the AIM market.

AIM's near-unique qualities

Historically the UK has a culture of supporting quoted smaller companies. From a UK perspective, it's easy to overlook the near-uniqueness of AIM. Its breadth and diversity sets it apart from almost every other developed market. Very few countries indeed, perhaps just the UK and Japan, have such highly developed universes of smaller listed companies. AIM is all the more unusual for the fact that it came into existence at a time when the wider trend was away from smallness towards supporting scale and globalisation. Others have sought to establish their own AIM-like exchanges but this proved near impossible during the credit boom.

So the AIM exchange stands as something of a beacon; an exchange that is dominated by smallness at a time when market trends are changing. Remember that AIM became established at a time when investors were reducing their holdings of smaller UK companies. It has come into existence during decades when smaller company indices have been underperforming emerging markets or speculative investments fuelled by the credit boom. It has survived and expanded despite the fact that many of its new issues have come to market at times of excessive optimism, leading to many IPO investors bearing disappointing returns.

Logically, AIM should have withered and died. Countless similar markets set up to provide capital to smaller quoted companies have done so, or been subsumed into larger entities and lost their identity. Where are the Nouveau Marché,[70] Neuer Markt[71] or EASDAQ[72] now? We are exceptionally fortunate that the long history of support for the smallest quoted stocks in the UK has resulted in AIM surviving when most others have foundered. When it comes to allocating capital to smallness, our public markets have had a culture of supporting companies that are rather smaller than elsewhere. Raising, say, £10m via public markets would be difficult or indeed impossible in many other countries around the globe, but not in the UK.

---

70   Nouveau Marché – France's stock market dedicated to small companies, subsumed into Euro.nm and since disbanded.

71   Neuer Markt – Germany's stock market dedicated to small companies, subsumed into Euro.nm and since disbanded.

72   Founded as a European alternative to NASDAQ. It was purchased by NASDAQ then closed in 2003 after the dotcom bubble burst.

Stocks quoted on AIM are superbly well-positioned to benefit from renewed focus on the positive characteristics of smallness, exhibiting features that have been proven to be powerful return generators in the past. Yes, from an investment perspective, there might be hurdles to overcome. Slow world growth and all sorts of economic and geopolitical setbacks will present major challenges to smaller companies as well as larger stocks. But it's the nature of those hurdles that keeps the investment landscape a little less crowded than elsewhere, and increases the chances of the small, nimble and well-capitalised delivering attractive returns over the coming years.

Conclusion

Although the tiniest companies frequently feature amongst the top stock market performers each year, often AIM-listed new issues have ultimately delivered disappointing returns. The negative cash flow of dotcom or unfunded resource exploration stocks means they suffer from the disadvantage of having a limited time frame to achieve success. But really successful investment is not just about trying to get lucky over a single year. It's about spotting the potential to make an attractive return over time, perhaps over years and years.

From this perspective, there are relatively few really small companies or businesses whose stocks are significantly mispriced on the LSE exchange. But AIM has plenty. These are genuinely small conventional companies with regular turnover, profits and cash flow that have been largely overlooked during the boom. Frequently their low valuations have inhibited their ability to raise as much additional capital as they wanted to invest.

But beyond the credit boom, their ability to offer better returns for investors will increase their access to additional capital, and increase their opportunity to invest, which together mean that their growth prospects could be transformed. This is particularly the case for the smallest ant-sized companies, especially those with plenty of tangible assets and strong balance sheets. These companies may not achieve the same instant share price gains as some more speculative stocks did during the boom, but many could have hugely attractive risk/reward ratios, and the ability to put new capital to work to generate productivity improvements. Companies like this can not only deliver attractive returns at a time when others might struggle, but also offer the scope to sustain such returns for several years in succession.

AIM came into existence at a time when the wider market trends favoured scale and globalisation. Government-sponsored VCT and EIS schemes helped it buck the wider trend through favourable tax incentives. This often kept AIM open even at times when the main market was suffering a pull back. It now stands as something of a beacon. For those looking to invest in genuinely small companies, it provides access to a wide-ranging universe of the smallest quoted stocks. In contrast, nearly all other exchanges are dominated by mid-sized or larger companies and therefore lack decent weightings in the smallest quoted stocks.

If the future is indeed small, AIM appears unusually well-positioned to participate in the new trends. All the evidence points to this being the start of a new super-cycle in smallcap returns.

CHAPTER 6
Smallness in Action

Domestic troubles: Creating jobs and increasing the tax take

The expansionary phase of the credit boom was a time of apparent plenty in which many economies around the world grew faster than the long-term average. In retrospect, we can now see that growth was significantly enhanced by the use of debt. Beyond the credit boom, we face the hangover, and economists are asking how we're going to create growth and jobs in the future. In a slower-growth world, where will the dynamism come from?

During the boom, tax take expanded significantly. As a result, many governments increased in scale and stepped up their own spending. In addition, with the cost of credit falling, their interest costs also fell, and they were able to spend a larger part of their revenues. The trends were so favourable that they typically boosted their financial commitments into the future as well. So in the run up to 2007, the UK's growth appeared noticeably faster than some of its European neighbours and the US. However, it looks rather less impressive if the strong rise in government spending after the millennium is excluded. As the next illustration shows, without it, the UK did not lead the pack of developed economies in growth terms at all. In fact, it lagged its major rivals.

Together, government spending and debt-driven consumption helped fuel the boom.

Using government spending
to drive growth

Growth drivers in the US, UK, France and Germany
Average annual GDP growth per capita 1993–2007

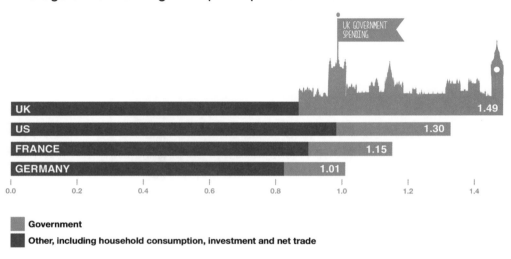

UK GOVERNMENT SPENDING

UK	1.49
US	1.30
FRANCE	1.15
GERMANY	1.01

0.0   0.2   0.4   0.6   0.8   1.0   1.2   1.4

■ Government
■ Other, including household consumption, investment and net trade

Source: CBI, *A Vision for Rebalancing the Economy: A new approach to growth*, UNCTAD

After the credit crisis in 2008, the UK economy contracted and tax take fell away, only returning to pre-crisis levels six years later. Although the UK budget deficit widened alarmingly just after the peak of the crisis, the hope was that the deficit would narrow as economic growth picked up again, along with government revenues.

But tomorrow's trajectory is far from certain. Remember that the post-crisis recovery has been much slower than in the past. Indeed, as the overall population of the UK has increased since 2008, the recovery looks something of a mirage when calculated with that factor in mind.[73] In addition, some of the key structural problems are yet to be addressed, particularly those that relate to the ageing population and the pressing need to improve the efficiency of the economy. In 2014, the average UK worker produced less in an hour of work than his counterparts in the US, Germany or France, and less than

---

73   Morning headlines, *MacroStrategy Partnership*, 20 August 2014.

in 2007 before the financial crisis.[74] Meanwhile official forecasts, such as those shown in the next illustration, assume a swift reversal of the trend and a comfortable uptick in efficiency in the future.[75] There's no escaping it – the economic challenge is immense.

UK budget deficit 2000–2018

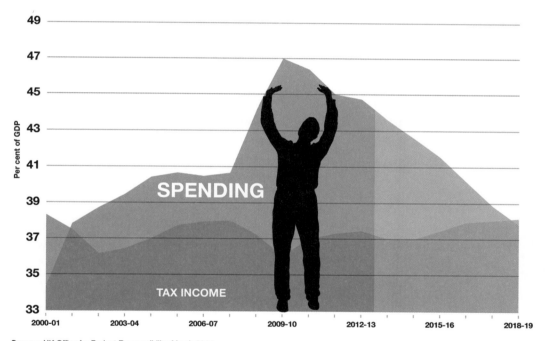

Source: UK Office for Budget Responsibility, March 2014

During the boom, the huge issuance of debt boosted economic activity as we borrowed growth from the future. Beyond the boom, we face the period of growth payback. Many banks over-expanded and have been forced to scale back their activities, shrinking their

---

74   Source: Output per hour, as calculated by the Office for National Statistics, 'Labour Productivity, Q1 2014'.

75   Morning headlines, *MacroStrategy Partnership*, 20 August 2014.

balance sheets. As debt is repaid, it has the effect of reducing economic activity, cutting demand for goods and services within the economy. The boom took two to three decades to peak, so it's logical to expect the economic imbalances it created to take a couple of decades to rebalance. This poses a major challenge for governments. It means that the gap between revenue received in taxed income and their spending *won't be closed by a rapid pick-up in the world economy*.

As we move beyond QE, governments will find it more difficult to finance their excess spending – it's going to be much harder to fix the problem of the budget deficit. Increasingly governments will be forced to reduce expenditure, and in many cases government jobs, despite the political disadvantages of unemployment. Sustainable job creation will become ever more central to the political agenda. In fact, post credit boom, it will almost certainly be the top political imperative.

So with government shrinking,[76] what actions can the administration take to help revitalise the economy and increase employment in the private sector? Many conventional stimulative policies have been used to exhaustion. Most economists and central bankers agree that cutting interest rates should help boost economic activity, yet with interest rates already at the lowest they have ever been since the Bank of England was established in 1694,[77] there's effectively no further scope to do so.

Since the 1960s, large companies have grown to play an increasingly powerful role in the global economy. Indeed, on a value-added basis, almost one third of the world's 100 largest economic powerhouses are companies, not countries[78] – so perhaps part of the solution is a more effective harnessing of the power of the corporation.

The role of multinationals

In recent years, given the uncertain times and lack of economic growth, many corporates have trimmed their operations and held back investment plans. Across the corporate sector worldwide, the numbers are colossal – billions of pounds are being held onto and not put to work in developing productive capacity. In this context, it's troubling to see how much corporate cash large companies have accumulated in the post-crisis years.

---

76   UK Office for Budgetary Responsibility (2014), 'Economic and Fiscal Outlook', March 2014.

77   Source: Bank of England.

78   Roach, R. (2007), 'Corporate Power in a Global Economy', teaching module at Global Development And Environment Institute, Tufts University.

Who has cash?

Selected US companies – holdings of cash and cash equivalents*

*Cash includes assets in checking deposits, currency deposits, term deposits and in money market funds

Source: U.S. Trust, Moody's Financial Metrics; IMF, April 2014

Coca Cola
$20bn

Johnson & Johnson
$29bn

Microsoft
$84bn

Ford
$25bn

Pfizer
$49bn

General Motors
$28bn

Apple
$159bn

So why are companies not using their cash more actively? Certainly, since 2008, there have been more economic unknowns, but could it also be that they are running low on ideas? Some economists are quite concerned by this, and highlight that worldwide innovation seems to be slowing. The trend can be identified quite clearly, running as far back as the early 1970s.[79]

And if you delve a little more deeply, it soon becomes clear that the gigantic corporate cash piles are – in aggregate – dwarfed by the mountainous stock of corporate debt that's been issued too. The trend was interrupted when the financial crisis of 2008 caught many of the gigantic companies out, but after 2009 it was re-established with a vengeance. Credit issuance by the corporate sector is higher than ever.[80]

Using QE for government-backed purchases of bonds and mortgage securities effectively created one-way bets in some asset markets. Without it, as QE starts to be wound down, there's a danger that asset prices become more volatile. In particular, there is a risk that the yields on some bond prices rise, making the issue price of corporate debt more costly. (Investors have already had a small taste of bond market volatility and rising yields in the discussions surrounding the tapering of QE.[81]) What this boils down to is critical: in future, when a corporate bond issue becomes due for repayment, the cost of *new* debt is likely to be higher than before. In other words, any firm reliant on credit will find that reliance much more expensive – perhaps unsustainably so. This is a significant challenge. The corporate bond market has been *extremely* active in the post-crisis years; around $8.9trn of corporate debt is coming due by 2018.[82]

Some large multinationals won't just have costlier corporate debt to deal with. Many such firms' debts were run up at a time when corporate profit margins in the UK and the US were unusually high (for reasons discussed in earlier chapters). As austerity bites and corporate margins normalise, some debt burdens will be out of line with the underlying profitability of the company and simply prove unsustainable. If these issues come to a head at a time of higher interest rates, and a general market reluctance to fund new debt, the implications aren't pretty.

If anything, many larger companies have become badly over-geared during the credit boom. Their ability to help our economies rebalance beyond the boom is therefore less

---

79   *Ibid.*

80   Hunt, A. (2014). 'The Threat of Deflation Returns – The New Battle for Price Stability', Andrew Hunt Economics, April 2014.

81   'Taper tantrums', *Financial Times*, 16 August 2013.

82   Including bonds, loans and revolving credit. Source: Standard & Poor's Global Fixed Income Research (2014), 'Global Corporate Issuers Face $8.9 Trillion In Rated Debt Maturities Through Year-End 2018', 14 March 2014.

than certain and likely to deteriorate. Given the scale of the corporate bond market, it seems entirely likely that it will become *more* difficult for larger multinationals to fund higher capital investment in the years ahead. Despite their cash balances, many multinationals may in fact become short of risk capital as QE declines.

Put simply, multinationals have their own excesses to address, and are therefore unlikely to be able to greatly assist governments in the creation of extra private sector jobs.

Creating employment

If job creation is high on the agenda, yet debt-laden large companies are unlikely to create significant numbers of new jobs in the years ahead, one possible course of action is to step up investment in genuinely small companies. After all, research has found again and again that smaller companies play a disproportionately large role in employment creation in relation to their size.

In the UK, research carried out at the University of Nottingham has concluded that almost two thirds of new jobs in an average year are created by smaller companies.[83] Small businesses drive job creation. Of course, not all modest-sized businesses succeed – many don't. Jobs are destroyed all the time in an overall process of 'churn', but the pace at which jobs are *created* by smaller firms significantly exceeds the rate at which they're destroyed. Nottingham's research showed that despite the level of job churn, the new posts lasted *just as long as those created by large corporations*. It also identified that new firms made significant contributions to productivity, as they explored different ways to be more effective than incumbents. (Remember that boosting productivity in the face of deteriorating demographics is a key priority for the future.)

These findings are not unique to the UK. In the US, the smallest small firms are also disproportionately responsible for creating new jobs. In a study running from 1976 to 2005, start-ups accounted for 3% of overall employment but almost 20% of gross job creation. In contrast, firms with 500-plus employees tended – on average – to be overall destroyers of jobs.[84] This will undoubtedly ring true for anyone who has worked in a gigantic organisation and seen just how much management effort is spent on reducing the headcount.

---

83   See Wright, P., Upward, R. and Hijzen, A. (2010), 'Job creation, job destruction and the role of small firms', Leverhulme Centre for Research on Globalisation and Economic Policy, *Oxford Bulletin of Economics & Statistics* (Blackwell).

84   Haltiwanger, J.C., Jarmin, R.S. and Miranda, J. (2010), 'Who Creates Jobs? Small vs. Large vs. Young?', National Bureau of Economic Research, working paper 16300.

So it would be unwise to count on corporate giants to create work. Small and innovative firms are the ones that will be creating jobs and generating dynamism in future. But ant-sized companies will be unable to play that role effectively if they find that they are starved of capital to fund their own development.

Private SMEs are predominantly financed by individuals or business angels, though bank funding does play a part too. Governments have encouraged banks to increase the availability of credit for smaller businesses. The problem is that most banks became overextended during the boom; there has been a regulatory tightening and many are now reducing the scale of their loan books.

Nevertheless, there is plenty of scope for governments to influence the availability of capital for smaller listed companies. The actions of professional investors can be influenced by relatively modest changes in the tax regime. Capital flows into larger quoted companies and their smaller competitors is dynamic; relatively minor changes to the tax treatment of one or other of these groups can have a significant effect on the way in which professional investors make their allocations. So a direct link can be made between the political imperative to create jobs and the scope for government to address it by adjusting policies to encourage the flow of institutional capital into quoted small and micro-cap stocks.

Governments have already implemented several policies to kick-start this process. Removing the stamp duty payable on the purchase of AIM shares, agreed in early 2013, will increase investment in smaller companies to some degree. According to the LSE, in time the knock-on effect might be more than 20,000 extra jobs.[85]

The psychological appeal of small

There are lots of rational reasons to increase support for small firms, but there's also something appealing about smallness on an emotional level. And there may be more to this than meets the eye.

Back in the 1970s, the radical economist Schumacher pointed out that comfort with the small and the personal was part of the human psyche – he believed that people are naturally drawn to smallness within a larger whole. Why? For Schumacher, it was all about "convenience, humanity and manageability".

---

85 'Abolishing stamp duty on AIM shares is a bold and decisive policy from government', London Stock Exchange, 21 March 2013.

In this context, it's intriguing to see anthropologists exploring whether there might be a limit to the number of meaningful connections that individuals can make based on the size of the brain. Their findings suggest that there may be cognitive limits to the size of human networks.[86] Based on brain size alone, anthropologists have suggested an optimal human group size of around 150.[87] Consider this in the light of the ideas emerging in development theory, highlighted in Chapter 3, where research has tried to establish at what stage of largeness organisations become less efficient. It's not very large at all. Research suggests that productivity can increase quite substantially in groups of up to 250, but above that number, productivity gains tail off.[88]

The ending of the recent credit boom may actually end up helping the perception of small businesses going forward. Following the crisis of 2008, it's become more apparent that super-scaled financial organisations can threaten economic stability precisely because of their outsize scale (and therefore outsize risks). There's been greater attention on how multinationals juggle their operations between different jurisdictions to avoid paying tax at a time when public finances are stretched. And there's been more focus on the distributional effects of advanced capitalism – where QE, for example, has benefited existing asset-holders disproportionately.[89] All of these features have helped make the corporate heel of big business less appealing.

These features have not been missed in the business world, at the organisational level or in the way in which businesses project themselves. As a result, some large and potentially impersonal organisations have been restructured into smaller or even semi-autonomous ones. Some are keen to suggest that they can be simultaneously vast, yet small and local – these are managed responses to concerns about gigantism. Exploring smallness within largeness is already underway.

Many UK consumers are now re-evaluating and prioritising British companies as a way of making a deliberate and active contribution to improve the health of the domestic economy. These actions can take place at many levels, from choices on consumption that prioritise goods made in the UK to selecting the companies for whom we choose to work. So far, though, the

---

86   Hill, R.A. and Dunbar, R.I.M. (2003), 'Social Network Size in Humans', *Human Nature* (Walter de Gruyter), vol. 14, no. 1, pp. 53–72. Note that the findings on average numbers within a social network in this research are based on a small sample size.

87   There are multiple features at work here, but 150 is now a frequent reference point used in social network design.

88   Soderbom, M. and Sato, Y. (2011), 'Are larger firms more productive due to scale economies? A contrary evidence from Swedish microdata', seminar at University of Gothenburg.

89   'The Distributional Effects of Asset Purchases', Bank of England, 12 July 2012.

growing appreciation of smallness in the UK has not had a major impact on globalisation, but there are some signs that the cross-border relationships that characterise the modern global economy may be peaking. It's certainly true that international connectedness has increased in recent decades, but the trend is not new. Past centuries have also seen waves of global integration which have then been disrupted, and there's no reason to believe that the same pattern won't repeat itself to some degree. Don't forget that individuals place a high value on the subtle differences that differentiate places and products from one another – attitudes to such differences can change remarkably rapidly.

These considerations are still immature in the investment world. Although over half of all UK households have savings and pensions that are managed by the UK fund management industry,[90] very few investors have played a significant role in deciding how their own savings should be allocated. Currently most are unaware of the proportion of their savings that is put to work outside the UK. Fewer still appreciate how much of their own capital backs ultra-large companies at the expense of small, or is being used to pursue transactional strategies.

As the UK moves ahead with auto-enrolment, where employers must ensure that all of their staff can join pension saving schemes, these issues are likely to become increasingly visible to savers. As the ultimate owners, savers are remarkably well-placed to at least question and perhaps exert some direct influence over how their own capital is allocated.

The question is how far this trend can develop. Hardly any institutions are overweight in small and micro-cap domestic stocks in 2014, but now that genuinely small companies have started to outperform, things will change. Institutional investors may not know it yet, but in time they will start to allocate a growing proportion of their capital to UK smaller companies. But this process will take many years. If extremes of asset allocation are a measure of the maturity of a trend, then it is clear that the smallcap pendulum is at a 25-year displacement from the previous norm. It is hard to anticipate change, but it will come. And as the new trend becomes established, the pendulum accelerates progressively.

Conclusion

The reliance on debt to drive growth has contributed to unhealthy imbalances in the domestic economy. Now that there is a long-term constraint on government spending, there's a pressing need to find new ways to generate dynamism in those parts of the economy that will be able to buck austerity in the years ahead. This priority is likely

---

90 *Key Facts about UK Financial and Related Professional Services*, TheCityUK, 6 January 2014, p.5.

to become all the more urgent as global productivity is flat-lining, with many larger companies cutting back on their capital expenditure. Indeed, many larger companies are so indebted that if asset prices were to fall they may have to redirect cash flow to fund interest rate payments or pay down excess debt.

In a slower-growth world, job creation will remain a top priority on the political agenda. But it is smaller organisations that play a disproportionately large role in generating new employment compared with bigger ones. Larger companies look for synergies through consolidation and often end up reducing net employment.

Individuals can have an impact on economic rebalancing by making a considered choice to prioritise smaller UK quoted companies. Backing smaller, domestic companies over a series of years can contribute to revitalisation of the economy. Re-engaging with smallness is appealing on a psychological level too; people like to feel they can make a real difference. As yet relatively few savers are expressing their opinions as to how they would like their capital to be allocated by their savings institutions. But in time there will be greater demand for more capital to be invested in smallcaps. And as auto-enrolment steps up participation in saving, this too will swell the numbers contributing to the debate about where our collective assets should be allocated.

The smallest domestic companies have already started to resume their previous trend of outperformance, in a similar way to the decades prior to the credit boom. Some worry that they may have missed the best of the gains. But if extremes of asset allocation are a measure of the maturity of a trend, then it's reassuring to note that the pendulum is still close to its maximum 25-year displacement. Hardly any institutions have decent weightings in small and micro-cap stocks.

All the factors point the same way. The trends in historic data, the need for the UK economy to rebalance, the government's focus on generating more employment, the need to boost domestic growth and corporate tax take, the renewed interest in re-engaging with businesses operating in the UK and widening participation in savings products. While institutional investors may not know it yet, in time they are likely to invest a growing proportion of their capital in genuinely small companies, or face underperforming the wider market for an extended period. A timely confluence of ideas will contribute to making the future small.

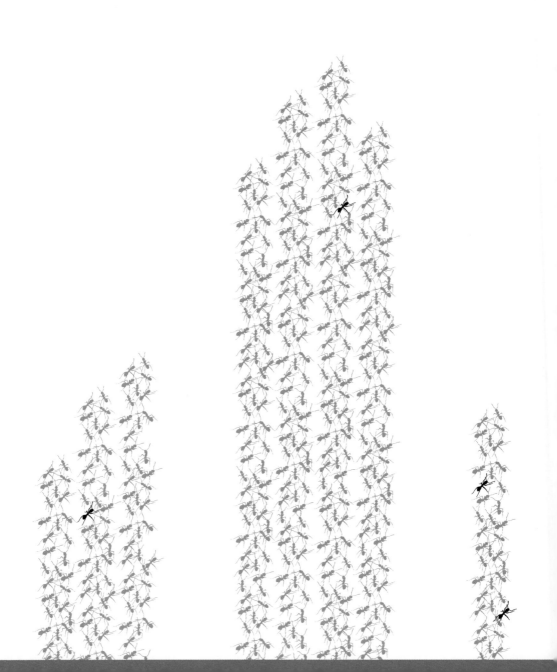

CHAPTER 7

How to Invest on AIM

The challenges of investing

If you have been convinced by the main thesis of this book and are considering investing in AIM, there's something important to have clear from the start – there are specific risks that come with investing in a junior market.

Many AIM-listed companies are young; they've come to the market in order to raise the finance they need to explore new prospects or develop ideas. Information on the companies themselves might be thin on the ground, and their skills at cash management will be critical. (AIM listing requirements include the need to provide three years of financial information prior to coming to the market; they don't include the need to show that the company is earning enough revenue to support at least 75% of its business, as on the main market.[91])

And you'll need to be comfortable with the way in which AIM stock prices can move quite abruptly. AIM stocks can move quite substantially over short time frames. It's not unusual for the market's top movers to gain or lose more than 25% in a day. And lower liquidity might mean that it's not always possible to buy or sell a position as rapidly as more commonly traded stocks.

---

91 'A guide to listing on the London Stock Exchange', London Stock Exchange (2010).

These characteristics are part of the nature of AIM. They also explain, of course, exactly what makes it a real stock-pickers' market. They are what makes investing in AIM-listed companies such an interesting prospect: you can get in the door early, or access shares when they have modest valuations. This is particularly the case since some smaller stocks trade relatively infrequently; the stock price might not reflect all of the recent news flow as accurately as companies that trade second by second. And as many AIM stocks are off the institutional radar due to their essential smallness, the market itself has the great advantage of not necessarily behaving in the same way as other more closely watched areas. AIM shares tend not to appear in the metrics followed by the large institutions, for example, which track how various assets are behaving in relation to each other. All the better for it!

Although AIM is relatively small, it is diverse. As well as having some of the UK's truly home-grown businesses listed on it, it features lots of smaller international companies who see the advantages of raising their profile in London. Within the ranks there are also companies that are now much larger in size – some valued at over £500m – which have chosen to remain on the junior market because they prefer its less onerous requirements to those of a senior listing.

Past performance

The challenges of investing in AIM-listed companies explain why many professional investors tend to avoid the very smallest, ant-sized companies. They are indeed often tiny, fiddly and have relatively modest analytical coverage. And as a group, AIM has made little headway since its inception; it certainly wouldn't be overstating the case to say that overall performance has been lacklustre. In fact, £100 invested in AIM back in 1996 would be worth just £89 in 2014.[92] This performance is all the more striking when seen in the context of other smallcap indices, such as the NSCI, illustrated in the next illustration. And it should certainly catch the attention of those seeking diversification, who appreciate how far many other credit-fuelled markets appear to be moving in tandem.

---

92   *Financial Times*, 19 January 2014.

Cumulative returns 1996–2013

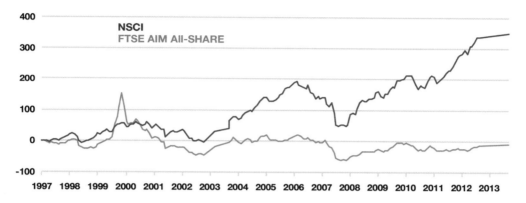

Source: Dimsom, E. and Marsh, P., as represented in *Numis Smaller Companies Index 2014 Annual Review*

So why has AIM failed to keep up with other smaller company indices and the main market? At different points since the mid-1990s it has been swamped by waves of enthusiasm; for technology companies, for resources stocks, for financial services firms. In each case, a series of mini-booms in IPO activity took place, with a great deal of excitement and interest inflating valuations. Stocks surged then peaked, typically quite dramatically, often presaging some extended periods of underperformance. These waves left investors who had chased the good news story of the day exposed when valuations fell post-IPO. And they often did.

It's true that most AIM stocks have not delivered attractive returns for their investors. But as we've explored in this book, they have a much better chance of delivering attractive returns going forward. Their distinctive features, particularly the scope that some smaller companies have to deliver in slower growth times, have not been at the forefront of minds and certainly not fully appreciated in the recent past. With credit abundant, and growth all around, it just hasn't been necessary to do so. It's interesting to note that many of the companies listing on AIM from 2013 onwards have moved to a significant premium in the IPO after-market. This is quite different to what occurred in the decade or so after the millennium.[93]

It's important to be aware of AIM's attributes, particularly if you have quite specific needs as an investor – for instance, as you approach retirement, or if you might require a lump sum at a particular point in the future. Remember that each year some stocks *delist* from AIM; delisting may hamper your ability to sell as and when you wish. That's the reality. So don't bank on the sale of a large holding of stock in a lesser-known, ant-sized company where the shares trade infrequently to fund a major financial commitment at a specific date in the future.

Whatever the case, the lacklustre headline performance of the AIM All-Share index conceals some very strong individual performances at the stock level every year. In 2013, for example, a handful of stocks more than doubled in value; many more gained over 50% in value. To be fair, 2013 was a good year for AIM, but double digit returns are not exceptional for the top performers in this market each year.

Preparing

When it comes to investing, the prepared prosper. Whether it's anticipating worst-case outcomes and planning how to react in advance, or just taking the time to work out what kind of investor they are, those who do their preparation are much more likely to come away from the markets smiling. The advice of this brief section could probably go for investing of all kinds, but it's still worth bearing in mind when heading into the world of the ant-sized AIM firm.

Most people think that investment decisions are largely rational. But while facts and figures clearly come into it, an investor's *emotions* are also incredibly relevant. It's easy to make rational decisions when things are going well. When things don't pan out as anticipated, it can be a different story. We're now much more aware of how far preconceptions cloud our decisions, and how we tend to seek evidence that supports our views.[94] This is the 'my-side bias', and why it's incredibly easy to let emotions get the better of us. Having a disciplined approach is absolutely essential. Given the volatility of AIM stocks, working out how you'll react to dramatic price spikes downwards is vital.

---

93   See comments on performance in the IPO after-market in the *Numis Smaller Companies Index Review 2014*, p.8.

94   Stanovitch, K.E., West, R.F. and Toplak, M.E. (2013), 'Myside bias, rational thinking, and intelligence', *Current Directions in Psychological Science*, vol. 22, no.4, pp.259–264.

To keep the process in perspective, anyone investing in AIM would be well advised to work out just what kind of investor they are before they begin. Then they can make sure that the approach that they take is absolutely appropriate, reflecting just how much time and energy they are prepared to invest.

For the legendary investor Benjamin Graham, there were three different types of investor:

- speculators
- active investors
- and passive investors.[95]

Speculators like quick capital gains, enjoy making decisions at speed and back their ability to trade out of positions quickly if things don't go as planned. **Active investors** are keen to engage more closely in the research process. They're interested in taking time to find the very best opportunities, and believe that more intensive research efforts might result in more lucrative returns. **Passive investors** moderate their ambition, steer away from stock-specific risk and expect no more than average investment returns. Inevitably this means a much lower degree of psychological involvement.[96] They're comfortable keeping their distance from stock selection and the investment process.

A perfect investment for a speculator is a stock that has been on a falling trend but then starts to pick-up again. The investor has a good reason for why the share price will keep on rising. Such investments can be vulnerable, though, so speculative investors are often momentum traders: ready to sell out if a trend changes. It's difficult to hold your nerve if the share price fluctuates daily, hitting a new high then dropping alarmingly. Is it time to sell or is it better to stay on-board in case the stock suddenly bounces back again? Most speculative investors either sell well before the share price peaks or well after it begins to slide.

Active investors tend to seek investments amongst those stocks that are out of fashion, perhaps when markets are weak. The active investor researches a range of companies, and narrows his or her interest down to those where the fundamentals suggest the business could be worth a lot more over the medium or longer term. When it goes right, it can go right for some time. Nevertheless, just like speculative investors, active investors rarely sell at exactly the right time. And if a share price falls away unexpectedly, the active investor can fall into the trap of thinking this merely makes it an even better buying

---

95   Graham, B. (1949), *The Intelligent Investor* (Harper & Row).
96   Further analysis can be found in Williams, G. (2011), *Slow Finance* (Bloomsbury).

opportunity. Many active investors continue to support the original thesis that drove an initial investment, and downplay any news that seems to run counter to it. If they do this repeatedly, they run a fair chance of making substantial losses.

In contrast, passive investors have little to fear regarding specific investments. In Graham's time, passivity simply meant buying the stocks in the Dow Jones Industrials Average in equal amounts. Today, it means worrying about which index to follow. But remember that the largest weighting within an index could be many times larger than the smallest index position, and that indices tend to be full of companies that have already performed well in the past. These can be stocks that tend to have less upside potential on account of their scale or perhaps on account of an already long history of success.

Allocation and taxation

So take time to evaluate the risks before you jump into AIM. Less-experienced investors may like to take some advice from an independent financial advisor (IFA). IFAs are regulated and, just like their name suggests, should be able to make proposals without being tethered by individual providers. When it comes to selecting an IFA, online services such as www. unbiased.co.uk or www.findanadviser.org can help. Make sure you select a specialist with expertise in your own area of interest – not every IFA will be able to cover all the bases. And be sure to cover off any questions on service levels and charges before you begin.

At the outset, you need to establish exactly what your priorities are in terms of your own investment goals and time horizons. If you are persuaded by the ideas set out in this book, give some careful thought as to how much of your portfolio you plan to invest in ant-sized firms and elsewhere. In percentage terms, some financial advisers recommend investing no more than around 5 to 10% of an overall portfolio in smaller and micro-sized companies, but there is no right answer or 'one size fits all' solution. The answer depends on your own situation, what kind of investment timescale you have in mind and – very importantly – your tax position.

Indeed, when it comes to tax, because the government has recognised how important smaller companies are, there are tax advantages to be had. Firstly, a lot of – but not all – AIM-listed stocks qualify for business property relief so are free of inheritance tax (IHT) if held for more than two years. (This only applies to those individuals who buy stocks directly, so funds investing in AIM stocks do not have this benefit.) To qualify, the companies in question need to be regular trading businesses, and not investment companies or similar. That's because the government is keen to ensure that any capital that is invested on this basis is directed into proper businesses rather than AIM-listed companies that don't carry any commercial risk. But be aware that HMRC does not issue a list of approved stocks, and will only confirm whether the holdings are IHT-free at the time of probate. However as long as the intentions of government are kept in mind, and most property and investment companies are avoided, then the decisions by HMRC to date seem to approve most AIM-listed stocks as free of IHT.

In addition, the rules around ISAs (individual savings accounts) have been changed to allow investors to buy AIM shares within these tax-free accounts (just as you have been able to buy shares in other markets). It's also possible to invest via venture capital trusts and enterprise investment schemes. So in principle, there are routes to invest in AIM-shares that can be free from income, capital gains and inheritance taxes.[97] Of course the ground rules around these structures are subject to change. Your IFA will be able to give more details, and guide you on exactly what's available in the market.

Once you know how you are planning to invest, what the worst-case might look like and are confident that you won't need immediate access to any funds that you're planning to invest – here's how to begin:

Investing through funds

The quite specific characteristics of AIM – including the lower information requirements on listing and lack of liquidity in some stocks – mean that investing collectively (in other words, through a fund) might be the most suitable route for those who want to keep a reasonable psychological distance or just don't have the time or inclination to get involved in managing a portfolio.

The same path is probably also the best for inexperienced investors. By investing in a fund or pooled investment, you get access to niche experience; the manager deals with diversification and liquidity issues, which are inevitably harder to manage in this part of the market. A fund also offers the convenience of being just one thing to monitor, rather than lots of individual companies. And if you make regular savings, for example on a monthly basis, you avoid some of the uncertainties relating to the inevitable peaks and troughs of the market and trying to identify the best points at which to invest. Your capital will be invested regardless.

---

97   Evans, R. (2013), 'Birth of the IHT-free Isa as ban on Aim shares is lifted', *The Telegraph*, 1 July 2013.

ACTIVE FUNDS

There are a handful of funds concentrating on the smaller or micro end of the market. In each case, the orientation and precise objectives of the fund will be set out in a simplified prospectus or key investor information document (KIID). Check the orientation of a fund's strategy carefully. It should set out exactly how smallness will be accessed. Remember that some benchmarks of smallness contain some much larger companies; even a number of professionally managed smaller company funds have moved away from the very smallest stocks, preferring to participate in the kind of medium-sized companies that outperformed ant-sized ones in the run-up to 2013. In the long run, history suggests that this could have performance implications, as returns from the very smallest and least liquid companies have tended to be greater than those from their larger counterparts – in spite of higher transaction costs. Check the data in Chapters 4 and 5 if you need to be reassured of this.

Fund selection is hugely important. This might seem so blindingly obvious that it's barely worth a mention, but the majority of active managers fail to outperform their benchmarks over ten years, and the divergence between the best and weakest fund managers can be quite substantial. In May 2014, for example, the divergence between the top performer and the tail end in the smaller companies' universe was more than 50% over one year![98] In this sector in particular, it might not be a matter of small differences. It can mean double digit differences in returns over a 12-month period. With this much divergence, it's worth spending time to make sure that you're with the right manager, with a fund that doesn't suffer from benchmark tyranny and invests in some of the smallest quoted stocks where growth potential may be the best.

PASSIVE FUNDS

On AIM, the opportunities for investment strategies based on tracking established stock market indices are quite constrained. There are no tracker funds or exchange-traded funds (ETFs) that follow AIM itself. The shares of many AIM companies trade relatively infrequently and it would be near impossible for a manager to access all the relevant stocks. There are trackers which follow other UK smallcap indices, such as the MSCI UK Small Cap index, but be aware that their universe of companies is dominated by larger weightings in those at the top of the index and sometimes they are trimmed to exclude the very tiniest companies.

---

98   Source: Barclays Stockbrokers, Fund Tools, Top Funds, UK Smaller Companies sector (as on 22 May 2014).

Investing yourself

Investors who relish the chance of setting their own investment agenda will need a UK stockbroker. You can find one – all of whom are regulated by the Financial Conduct Authority – through the LSE website.[99] Or, if you feel comfortable handing the reins to someone else entirely, there are a large number of discretionary brokers able to make decisions on your behalf.

Of course, it's not the case that everyone wants or needs the same level of input. If you feel that you don't need advice, execution-only brokers will carry out your instructions; if you need a little more guidance, advisory brokers can help. There is also a range of execution-only websites too. Technology has not only greatly reduced costs but also provides an easy way to keep abreast of share price movements in your portfolio stocks. Being an immature market, it's worth comparing the quarterly costs on several before choosing one – they do vary considerably.

Principles guiding stock-picking

When it comes to stock-picking, I am an advocate of Benjamin Graham's approach. Graham is the author of perhaps the definitive text on value investing.[100] Initially working from his experience of investing in the 1930s, Graham set out a strategy that should deliver even when markets are flat. In the light of the economic uncertainties set out in Chapter 1, this has obvious appeal today.

Graham advocated seeking conservatively valued companies and buying stocks when they are intrinsically cheap. What he meant by this was to ensure that the price at which a stock was bought – and therefore by extension the implied valuation of the company – was less than could be raised by closing the business and selling off its assets. These tend to be companies that are generally thought to have relatively unexciting prospects for a variety of reasons. Needless to say, there are not so many modestly valued companies around now, particularly as so many valuations seem to have come untethered from underlying earnings in recent times. Nevertheless, the key point is that Graham recognised the disappointments that can follow if your strategy relies on chasing stocks where success is *already baked into the price*. He didn't support buying front runners.

---

99   www.londonstockexchange.com/traders-and-brokers/traders-brokers/home.htm

100   Graham, B. (1949), *The Intelligent Investor* (Harper & Row).

In simple terms, Graham sought assets that might be worth £1 but could be bought at just 50p. He sought companies that were so conservatively valued there was a clear margin of safety in investing in them. Although stock prices might move around every day, sometimes quite dramatically, the margin of safety would act as a kind of insurance policy, insulating the investor from any further decline in stock price. And if a stock *was* fundamentally undervalued, there was a reasonable chance that it would move up and revert closer to fair value at some point in the future.

Throughout a successful lifetime of investing, Graham progressively simplified his approach. By his retirement in the 1950s, he was able to offer investors some essential pieces of advice based on his own observations – and they're worth repeating.

Firstly, he rejected short-term speculation in favour of making clear and consistent value investments, based on straightforward processes and assessments. He saw no need for what he called "elaborate techniques".[101] Instead, he proposed targeting stocks trading at less than the value of their working capital, i.e. the value of current assets minus the value of current liabilities. Other potential targets included stocks trading at less than seven times the level of reported earnings over the previous 12 months or able to sustain dividend yields above 7%, calculated by dividing dividends per share by price per share. The latter is a way to measure just how much cash is being generated by each pound invested.

When building a portfolio, once again he advocated diversity and simplicity, ensuring that no single investment would have an overly large impact on the performance of the whole. Then, when it came to guidance on when to sell, Graham recommended having a defined policy in place, with an explicit stock target price agreed over a set time period. If that target price was not met within two to three years, he proposed that the investment should be sold.

Finally, he maintained that a percentage of the overall portfolio should be kept in 'safe' bond or bond-like assets and to increase or reduce the amount of capital invested in shares to profit from market setbacks. He suggested not allowing the minimum allocation in either class to fall below 25% of the total portfolio. That switching between assets of course means buying when the rest of the market is fearful and reluctant to do so, taking advantage of subdued valuations at times of market distress.

I'll address each of these points in turn. As a long-term strategy, value has certainly proved its worth. First advocated many years ago, its effectiveness has been explored very

---

101   See interview reprinted in the *Financial Analysts Journal*: **www.bylo.org/bgraham76.html**

extensively by academics over the years. As an investment theme, value has outperformed significantly over long timescales, not just in the UK. Taking data from 23 stock markets around the world over a 39-year period between 1975 and 2013, value stocks outperformed stocks with growth characteristics by 2.3% each year;[102] since 2000, the outperformance has been even greater – on average, 3.1% each year. That outperformance across many of the world's stock markets is shown in the next illustration.

If you need to revisit the characteristics and past performance of the kinds of stocks that fall into the value and growth categories, you can find the details in Chapter 4. We now know that the value premium is greatest amongst smaller companies, not large ones, and this particular area is where I like to focus my attention. Combining the two features can be highly effective.

The value premium

Annualised premium in 23 countries 1975–2013

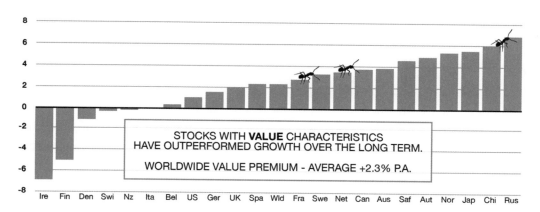

STOCKS WITH **VALUE** CHARACTERISTICS HAVE OUTPERFORMED GROWTH OVER THE LONG TERM.

WORLDWIDE VALUE PREMIUM - AVERAGE +2.3% P.A.

Source: MSCI Barra Value and Growth Indices
Cited in Dimson, E., Marsh, P. and Staunton, M. (2014), *Credit Suisse Global Investment Returns Sourcebook* (London Business School)

---

102 Dimson, E., Marsh, P. and Staunton, M. (2014), *Credit Suisse Global Investment Returns Sourcebook 2014* (Credit Suisse AG), p.48.

As I explained in *Slow Finance*,[103] it is incredibly difficult to pick out-and-out winners on the stock market, the kind of companies that deliver legendary performance on a case-by-case basis. But the appeal of Graham's approach lies in the way in which it should ensure a degree of insulation from the vagaries of the market. It gives some insulation from market volatility. This has always been important, but may become more so in the future, as analyses of economic performance, such as those carried out by the Economic Cycle Research Unit, suggest the prospect of higher volatility in the years ahead.[104]

The approach advocated by Graham later in his life seems particularly relevant for small and micro caps, where data might be scarce. So rather than embarking on detailed calculations integrating numerous variables for each potential company in which I might invest, I take a more holistic approach. **I track the prospects for increasing turnover, look at the potential to sustain or improve margins and how much headroom there is on the balance sheet.**

As outlined in Chapter 4, monitoring the balance sheet, particularly the proportion of debt and risk capital, is very important. Value investors focus on stocks that, for various reasons, are not regarded as having exciting prospects in the short term. Then, if they happen to exceed those modest expectations, there's a better chance of the stock moving higher and reverting closer to the mean. But any company whose prospects appear unexciting because it's overloaded with debt carries the risk that the equity return might be heavily diluted by new share issues, perhaps at a distressed price in the future, or that the entire company fails.

So, like Graham, I focus on **cash generation** and the **value of tangible assets**. For those with industrial assets, I tend to check on the insured value of assets, which can give quite an insightful snapshot of the cost that a new business would have to spend to enter their market. The **depth of experience of the management team** is hugely important too. Getting to really know the people making the decisions helps me get a better understanding of the risks and opportunities in each individual investment, and gives me greater confidence at times when the share price might fall away at times of market stress.

Of course, as market conditions have changed, some of the individual metrics flagged by Graham to identify potential targets are simply no longer appropriate. After the credit crisis, many stocks have appreciated quite significantly and appear to be trading higher than

---

103 Williams, G. (2011), *Slow Finance* (Bloomsbury).

104 Economic Cycle Research Unit (2014), 'Cognitive Dissonance at the Fed?', 30 May 2014.

their intrinsic worth, and very few indeed are yielding anything close to Graham's target. Nevertheless, it is possible to pursue a slightly altered approach based on relative value.[105]

Dividend yield remains very significant. It can be an equally valid method of identifying the way in which the stock market might be intrinsically undervaluing stocks. Using measures like the earnings/price ratio (EPR), which illustrates what would be paid out if all earnings were distributed, we can concentrate on those firms able to pay good and growing dividends. The scope for investment income to grow through compounding is powerful, yet almost certainly underestimated in periods when asset prices appreciate rapidly. Take an initial investment of £20,000, for example, invested in a company with a dividend yield of 5%. If the company also manages to grow its income by 5% each year, the stock will appreciate. And if dividend income is reinvested each year for ten years, the initial £20,000 investment will be worth more than £51,000 a decade later. That illustrates exactly why the power of compounding shouldn't be ignored.

Research into higher yield strategies suggests that they make sense from a risk perspective too, being lower risk than low- and zero-yield strategies.[106] Although it's not quite clear why this might be the case – perhaps because investors simply persist in overpaying for growth – it does seem as if a regular cash dividend is much more valuable to investors than expectations of returns that might be received at some point in the future, always assuming that markets remain at their current levels.[107]

One important point to acknowledge is that Graham became more cautious about stock-picking as areas of the market became more heavily researched. In my view, this is one reason why working in some of the less heavily populated parts of the market makes sense. That is exactly what investing in ant-sized firms, not immediately excluding those with lower liquidity characteristics, allows you to do.

When it comes to selling, I diverge from Graham's view. Rather than targeting a holding period of just two or three years (as he proposed), some of my most successful investments have been held for over ten years. My longest holding period is perhaps around the 15-year mark. I do of course review my holdings regularly as the prospects for a business often diverge from my assumptions. I have to be disciplined in checking

---

105   Value assessed in the light of similar assets; contrasting with absolute value which assess intrinsic features.

106   See Dimson, E., Marsh, P. and Staunton, M. (2014), *Credit Suisse Global Investment Returns Sourcebook 2014* (Credit Suisse AG), p 51. Reference to 2011 study covering 23 countries measuring average beta i.e. systematic risk.

107   Arnott, R., Li, F. and Sherrerd, K. (2008), 'Clairvoyant Value and the Value Effect', Research Affiliates.

that I stay invested for all the right reasons. If the turnover of a business starts to fall, or its profit margins turn out to be unsustainable, often the prospects for further share price appreciation is lost. Long-term investors should be aware that it can be wise to change your view if the fundamental trends in a business change meaningfully.

Graham set a high stock on capital preservation. For that reason, I feel his proposal of maintaining at least 25% of a portfolio in defensive assets is actually too extreme. At times when markets have already sold off aggressively, the risk/reward ratio for investors into really well-financed smaller companies can be a lot better than most fear. Certainly in the early part of 2009 I felt it was advisable to take on rather more risk than most felt was comfortable. For our professional portfolios we rarely use borrowing facilities, but at that time we moved to our maximum permitted borrowing.[108]

Diversification is always important and sometimes doesn't get the attention it deserves. Many professional investors explicitly advise against those with limited experience investing in just a handful of smaller companies, particularly when limited data is available. The overall risks involved can turn out to be much greater than assumed, and lost capital is often hard to recoup. My view is that around 25 largely equally weighted holdings within a portfolio should be sufficient to spread stock-specific risk, as long as the individual risks within each are not replicated across several holdings. Some value investors suggest that this could fall to as little as perhaps eight or ten holdings for experienced investors, but I strongly advocate a higher number. This gives the security of a better safety buffer should events turn for the worse in one or more of the investments.

Conclusion

There are cogent reasons why inexperienced investors might feel slightly cautious of AIM. In some cases there's limited stock available, which can inhibit the ability to trade freely and mean that, when sentiment changes, stock prices can reverse quite dramatically. Nevertheless, despite the volatility risks, there are plenty of advantages that come from investing in a diverse area of the stock market where the potential for dynamism and productivity enhancement appear to be better than most others.

---

108 Borrowing is possible in an investment trust structure, a closed-ended investment vehicle, but not in the open-ended unit trust structure, which is now more common. In 2009, the author was employed at Gartmore, responsible for the Gartmore Growth and Irish Growth Trusts, among others.

There's much greater scope to add value through stock selection in less-scrutinised areas of the market. Like Benjamin Graham, I keep the principles for stock selection simple, and focus on undervalued opportunities defined by intrinsic value and dividend yield. I keep a close eye on the headroom on the balance sheets and, from my experience in the past, am wary of companies that may have overextended themselves. But, unlike Graham, I sometimes hold stocks for years and years if the investment case is right and the operational climate remains positive.

From an investment perspective, it's encouraging to see how much the characteristics of companies coming to market for new listings have now changed. Unlike those who rushed for an AIM listing in the IPO-surges of the past, many now have solid cash-generative positions and scope to invest and deliver productivity improvements over the longer term. But the very fact that the AIM exchange itself hasn't risen since it was first established almost two decades ago is quite startling in the context of what has taken place in other asset markets in the same period. Successful investing takes time and needs close attention, and there will be all sorts of disappointments along the way. But in contrast with the past, my view is that a portfolio of carefully selected AIM stocks offer attractive returns in a way that is very different from most other segments of the market.

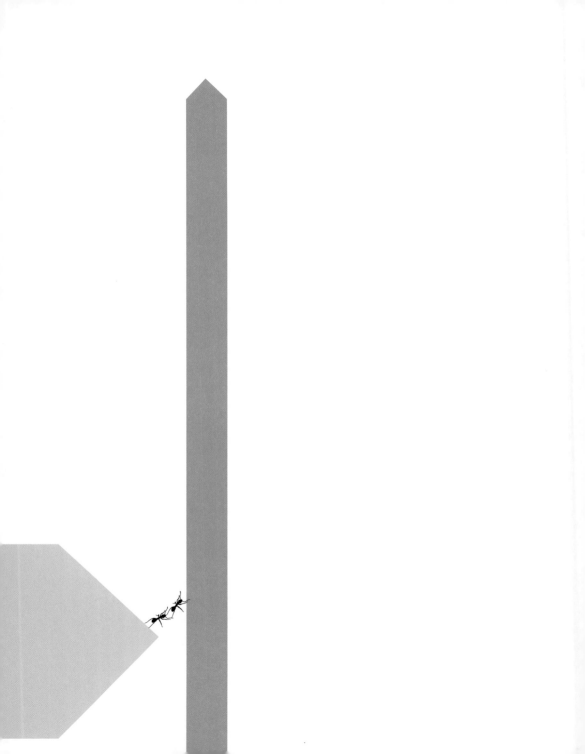

CHAPTER 8

Capital in Context

Why yesterday's strategies can't last

The financial crisis in 2008 was so serious that governments and central banks were forced to adopt emergency policies. In order to prevent a chaotic deflation of a global credit bubble that had been decades in the making, it was necessary to inject a giant surge of liquidity into the world economy through radical action. This has resulted in the financial markets staging a substantial and extended recovery.

One particularly unfortunate side effect has been that many of those that took on excessive debt during the boom haven't necessarily recognised the scale of their balance sheet risks. Although investors were initially spooked by the crisis, and there was potential for a major change in culture at the time, the subsequent market recovery has meant most have reverted to their previous practices. Credit boom strategies are once again delivering capital gains whilst those taking a more prudent approach might feel that they are missing out in the short-term, albeit to a lesser degree than the past (some strategies that delivered sizable profits during the boom are struggling).

With the market recovery from 2008 having gone on for years, the momentum for cultural change appears to have stalled. Some even believe that the inflated level of the financial markets is underwritten by central bank policies. 'Don't fight the Fed', they say, as they continue to pursue speculative strategies.

But despite full-bore QE applied over many years on an extraordinarily large scale, the injection of capital has failed to stimulate renewed world growth. The US was amongst the first to adopt QE, and has supplemented it with super-low interest rates along with tax concessions, and yet it has not enjoyed a significant acceleration in growth. In 2014, the Economic Cycle Research Unit – acknowledged experts in long term economic trends – described the US economy as running "below stall speed".[109] It anticipates lower growth, more recessions and higher volatility in the future. These issues are not just challenges to the US. Across the globe, most economies continue to lack economic vitality. The top seven developed economies grew just 0.4% in the first half of 2014.[110] (And that's despite ongoing stimulus, low interest rates, plus including an uncharacteristically strong one-off fillip in the UK as banks refunded PPI premiums of around £24bn to consumers.)

So the recovery of the financial markets feels out of step with the trajectory of real economies; asset markets seem to have become detached from fundamental economic dynamics. Over the two and half years up to the middle of 2014, expectations for corporate earnings have fallen sharply while equity market indices have remained on an upward trend. With inflationary pressures remaining very low, bond prices have risen too, and underlying bond yields have fallen towards record lows.

The extra market liquidity means that larger quoted corporates are finding it easy to issue yet more corporate debt. But generally these proceeds are not being invested to increase productivity. Instead, many larger corporates are issuing extra debt to fund buy-backs of their own shares.[111] This might increase the key earnings per share calculation on their businesses, closely watched for compensation purposes, but at a cost of raising their vulnerability to a future crisis. As the economist Andrew Hunt points out, US corporate indebtedness has moved to record levels, with debt issuance running at five times the post-war average.[112] The fall in bond yields has even reignited the opportunity for the least creditworthy companies to issue extra debt – the scale of the traded junk bond market has doubled in size since the credit crisis.[113]

So while the banks were at the epicentre of the financial crisis in 2008 and are undergoing a profound change of culture subsequently – withdrawing capital from investment banking, shrinking their loan books and so on – there is little cultural change in other parts of the financial sector. What financial participants may not realise is that market strategies based upon yesterday's trends are well past their sell-by dates. QE may be

109 Economic Cycle Research Unit (2014), 'Cognitive Dissonance at the Fed?', 30 May 2014.

110 Hunt, A. (2014), *Weekly Global Review*, 15 August 2014. Calculated on a weighted average basis.

111 'US share buybacks and dividends hit record', *Financial Times*, 18 June 2014.

112 Hunt, A. (2014), 'Can the FRB Afford to Tighten? Will it Do So Anyway?', *Weekly Global Review*, 4 July 2014.

113 'Junk Bonds at $2 Trillion as Gundlach Pulls Back: Credit Markets', *Bloomberg*, 19 March 2014.

smoothing the financial turning point but it isn't the solution. Real, sustainable, long-term wealth is not built upon clever trading, but on people working together to become more productive. The speculative may be able to spot an undervalued situation and capture a quick capital gain. But such gains are surely only illusory if the underlying asset doesn't have a fundamental capacity to offer greater utility in the future.

The future will be different. We face a profound change of culture right across the financial sector, with a much greater focus on investment strategies that 'look through' to the true nature of underlying assets and how their utility might be improved. Productivity improvements and their translation into tangible cash flow will become the real measure of progress in the future.

The relevance of genuinely small companies

It's all very well for a book like this to opine on the need for cultural change in the financial markets. Improvements in our productive capacity might seem rather esoteric at times when market returns have been so much better than inflation. The need for change can look rather theoretical. But market trends have already changed in a subtle way that's largely unnoticed. The FTSE 100 has struggled to break its pre-2000 peak, despite years of inflationary price increases. And although many of the credit-boom sectors led the market rally between 2009 and the early part of 2011, it has since been led by income stocks that normally lag strong rises in the market indices. Perhaps of greatest interest is the fact that genuinely small companies have started to outperform again.

This is making it harder for funds dedicated to sectors like mining, oil exploration and emerging economies to make progress. They have hardly participated in the market rally up to the middle of 2014. Equally, the daily turnover on shares on the LSE has reduced by around half since it peaked in 2006/2007, in spite of the sizable rise in the market.[114] Most unusual. This has made it more costly for traders to transact, and sometimes they can't complete their trades at all. Many hedge funds relying on transactional strategies have not been able to deliver the kinds of returns they generated previously.

None of these changes has been so momentous as to cause investors to radically change their investment strategies so far. At this stage they are merely facing lesser absolute performance rather than negative returns. It is difficult for professional investors to move away from a consensus that has been in place for nearly 30 years. Moving away

---

114 Datastream, Redburn, 2014.

requires great confidence that the previous consensus is no longer tenable – those who move ahead of the crowd and find the market recovers again can look foolish for a time. And few professional investors have a strong conviction that genuinely small companies will outperform over the coming decades. Not only have they generally underperformed for most of the last 25 years,[115] but by their nature they are illiquid too. If exchanges become more risky as QE is wound down, it seems almost perverse to consider moving capital away from the most liquid stocks, where it's relatively easy to adjust an investment stance should unexpected events unfold.

But the point about genuinely small companies is that they are in the business of change and more especially in increasing productivity. In this regard they are fundamentally different from larger stocks – some prosper at times and in places where the largest struggle. The analogy with ants in this book is not just decorative. Ant colonies are all about industrious activity on a genuinely small scale and how this contributes towards the benefit of the whole. Although ants are all around us, we rarely give them a thought. In the same way, most investors concentrate on the big and obvious – the largest stocks, the mainstream indices. But, as in the natural world, smallness is the foundation for everything else.

When genuinely small companies are well-funded, with good access to extra risk capital, it enables their management teams to pursue plans that can scale up their market positions and boost employment creation along the way. Since most genuinely small businesses are domestically focused, when they do succeed in achieving growth, they bring buoyancy. And remember, genuinely small companies don't tend to be sophisticated when it comes to tax. Most pay corporation tax to the government, so a vibrant universe of genuinely small companies increases the tax take of governments too. In the same way that the krill in the oceans are the foundation for the rest of the ecosystem, the ants of the quoted markets are the foundation for improving corporate productivity and facilitating wealth-generation.

What is remarkable about our current financial turning point is that professional investors still have exceptionally low weightings in genuinely small domestic quoted companies, entirely at odds with the long-term trends. Many professional investors now comfort themselves that the outperformance of smaller companies is a trend concentrated into shorter periods when three domestic factors are at work: at times when the UK economy is relatively buoyant, interest rates are falling (or low for longer periods), or when investors have greater confidence to take-on additional portfolio risk. At these times it is

---

115 As benchmarked by the FTSE SmallCap index, excluding investment companies.

easy to see why investors might prefer companies with a greater domestic bias. But all of these factors have been in place over recent years, and therefore some investors believe that these features wholly explain the recent outperformance of smaller stocks.

Despite the beguiling nature of these arguments, they do not stand up to scrutiny. Following the European Exchange Rate Mechanism crisis in 1992, the UK economy enjoyed its longest uninterrupted period of economic growth ever. Interest rates have fluctuated over the last three decades, but the direction of travel has been firmly downwards. And the phase has been marked by an increase in market participants employing more speculative strategies. Yet UK smaller companies generally underperformed for most of those decades. Other factors drive the outperformance of smaller quoted companies. We need to look back a little further in time.

The decades prior to the most recent credit boom were marked by a series of recessions in the UK. They included two oil price shocks leading to unusually high inflation in the 1970s. They also included phases when many UK businesses were paralysed by wide-ranging strike action, to the degree that the UK was described as 'the sick man of Europe'. The period even included the collapse of the pound, which required an emergency loan from the International Monetary Fund,[116] much like Ukraine in 2014 or Greece in 2010. And yet in these decades, smaller quoted companies outperformed by a wide margin.

The nexus in AIM

We need to be entirely clear here. Larger companies do have a hand in increasing the well-being of a nation. They form a major part of every national economy and employ sizeable workforces. Investment portfolios will continue to finance major businesses. This won't change. But a larger part of the innovation and vigour that drives productivity improvements within the economy comes from those that are smaller. In particular, it's often the case that the very small have more vitality than the merely small, and very much more vitality than the mid-scaled or larger corporations.

Smallness within the LSE listed universe has declined markedly during the credit boom. In this context, the AIM exchange is something of a beacon; an exchange that retains a wide-ranging community of genuinely small quoted companies at a time when most other exchanges dedicated to smallness have greatly reduced in scale or disappeared entirely. Of course, this does reflect some transfer of smaller quoted companies from LSE

---

116 UK National Archives, IMF Crisis: **www.nationalarchives.gov.uk/cabinetpapers/themes/imf-crisis.htm**

listings onto AIM. It should also be recognised that many of the new flotations on AIM haven't always delivered attractive returns; during the period of credit boom investors often preferred backing smaller companies that were more speculative. Even so, the AIM exchange has acted as a kind of Noah's Ark for the genuinely small corporate fauna during the credit boom decades. This isn't just down to the AIM exchange's own actions. We are collectively indebted to those individuals who persuaded government to keep the VCT and EIS schemes commercial at a time when they were deeply unfashionable in the financial sector. Although relatively modest in overall scale, their capital flows were sufficient to keep funding open for genuine smallness on AIM when many other junior markets were shrinking toward nothingness.

So beyond the credit boom, at the start of a period of renewed smaller company outperformance, the AIM universe of quoted smaller companies provides a wide ecosystem for capital to back. Renewed allocations to smallness may be modest initially but will become much more marked as the vulnerability of credit boom strategies becomes more obvious. It will take years for institutions to fully re-weight their UK portfolios into genuinely smaller companies, but their flow of capital and others' will boost the valuations of those with the best opportunities. Institutions may have grown to fear the illiquidity of quoted smaller companies because unwanted positions have been difficult to sell during the credit boom. But they may learn to fear illiquidity in the future for a different reason. If the future is indeed small, they may find it difficult to get their increased capital allocations invested in an illiquid sector that is progressively outperforming.

However, the established nature of the AIM exchange is a great advantage. By virtue of its continued survival, it has become one of the leading, maybe *the* leading exchange, of its kind in the world. We in the UK are profoundly lucky to have it, because it is full of industrious and vibrant activity. The benefits of having AIM in future won't just relate to the fact that many of its stocks are well-placed to deliver premium returns beyond the credit boom. The change in allocation will also contribute to the rebalancing of the UK economy. Clearly some individual businesses will be more successful than others, and some might not succeed at all, but the established nature of the AIM exchange makes this process much quicker to develop. Investment in this area of the markets will be differentiated in its commercial impact both short and long-term.

The developed nature of AIM won't just be relevant to accelerating the access to capital for UK businesses. Given the absence of international markets for smallness after the boom, the AIM exchange will be attractive to businesses looking for a listing from overseas too. Already there are over 250 companies incorporated outside of the UK with AIM quotes. These include some close to home, such as the Channel Islands – technically these territories are external to the UK and aren't actually in the EU either. But more importantly, it also includes quite decent numbers from Australia, Canada and South Africa, as well as more recent arrivals from other European countries and the US too. At the time of writing there are companies from 26 different countries listed on the exchange. Investors looking for a combination of the advantages of smallness will also be able to gain greater diversification through potentially including some of the international stocks in their portfolio too. If AIM sustains its leadership as an exchange that can match investors with genuinely small companies looking for capital, then the international listings will become much more substantial in time too.

Over recent years it seems that the market returns and investment flows within the City have become entirely separate from general trends in our economy. But the allocation of capital does not take place in a vacuum. Those who allocate a portion of their savings to the genuinely small have a direct effect on the productivity and well being of the wider community. The obvious benefits brought by the growth of smaller listed companies mean that there is already a wide-ranging political consensus favouring them. Changes such as allowing AIM-listed stocks to be included in ISAs[117] and removing stamp duty[118] ensure that the changes in capital allocation are accelerated by the improved returns through investing in these types of companies.

This is not to deny that there aren't risks that come from investing in a junior market – the illiquidity, the scope for things to go wrong and the fact that management teams can suffer bad luck. Not at all. But isn't it reassuring to find that the factors that are now driving the allocation of our savings are becoming realigned with the interests of the wider public again? That's because investing in the genuinely small is distinctive in its linkage with domestic investors.

The book begins with an analogy about an anthill covered in pine needles that, like AIM, is teeming with industrious activity that most overlook. Of course, AIM is that anthill. It's probably the best anthill I have ever come across. In a world of challenge, it fosters a large number of genuinely small companies full of potential productivity and vibrancy. These companies are the key to rebalancing the supply-side of our economy. And together their potential will drive the new super-cycle of investment returns in the coming years and decades.

---

117 See Chapter 7.
118 Purchase tax usually paid at the time of buying a quoted stock.

Bibliography

Chapter 1

'Global debt exceeds $100tn as governments binge, BIS says', *Bloomberg*, 9 March 2014.

Caruana, J. (2014), 'Global liquidity: where it stands and why it matters', Bank for International Settlements, IMFS Distinguished Lecture, Goethe University.

Cecchetti, S.G., Mohanty, M.S. and Zampolli, F. (2011), 'The real effects of debt', Bank for International Settlements, Working Paper 352.

Davies, G. (2014), 'The economic future of the Americans – some arithmetic', *ft.com*

Day, P. (2005), 'Banking's Long Revolution', *BBC News*: news.bbc.co.uk/1/hi/business/4604379.stm

Fisher, I. (1933), 'The Debt-Deflation Theory of Great Depressions', *Econometrica*, 1, iv.

Goodheart, C. in (2009), 'Banking Crisis: Dealing with the failure of the UK banks', Treasury Select Committee, *Seventh Report of the Session 2008–2009* (House of Commons), p.9.

Gordon, R.J. (2012), 'Is US economic growth over? Faltering innovation confronts the six headwinds', *Centre for Economic Policy Research* (Northwestern University and CEPR), *Policy Insight*, no. 63.

Harvey, D. (1990), *The Condition of Postmodernity: An enquiry into the Origins of Cultural Change* (Blackwell).

Hunt, A. (2014), 'The Threat of Deflation Returns – The New Battle for Price Stability', Andrew Hunt Economics.

Knox, R.E. and Inkster, J.A. (1968), 'Post-decision dissonance at post time', *Journal of Personality and Social Psychology*, 8, pp.319–323. Cited by Wilson, G. (2013), 'The Psychology of Money', lecture at Gresham College, London.

Nationwide House Price Index: www.nationwide.co.uk/about/house-price-index/download-data#tab:Downloaddata

Reinhart, C.M. and Rogoff, K.S. (2009), *This Time is Different* (Princeton University Press).

Summers, L. (2013), Speech given at IMF Economic Forum, Washington DC, 8 November 2013.

Turner, A. (2014), 'Escaping the Debt Addiction: Monetary & Macro-Prudential Policy in the Post-Crisis World', Center for Financial Studies.

Chapter 2

Citibank Investment Research and Analysis (2008), 'The law of large numbers', 30 June 2008.

Investment Management Association.

Lent, A. (2014), 'Small is Powerful: Escaping the 20th century love of big power', RSA, 15 June 2014.

Power, M., Ashby, S. and Palermo, T. (2013), *Risk Culture in Financial Organisations: Final Report* (Financial Services Knowledge Transfer Network).

Schumacher, E.F. (1973), *Small is Beautiful* (Blond and Briggs).

Chapter 3

Banz, R. (1981), 'The relationship between return and market value of common stocks', *Journal of Financial Economics*, 9, pp.3–18.

Dimson, E., Marsh, P. and Staunton, M. (2002), *Triumph of the Optimists: 101 Years of Global Investment Returns* (Princeton University Press).

Dimson, E., Marsh, P. and Staunton, M. (2014), *Credit Suisse Global Investment Returns Sourcebook 2014* (Credit Suisse AG).

Dimson, E. and Marsh, P. (2014), *Numis Smaller Companies Index Annual Review 2014* (Numis Securities).

Ibbotson, R.G., Chen, Z., Kim, D.Y-J., Hu, W.Y. (2013), 'Liquidity as an Investment Style', *Financial Analysts Journal*, vol. 69, no. 3.

Soderbom, M. and Sato, Y. (2011), 'Are larger firms more productive due to scale economies? A contrary evidence from Swedish microdata', seminar at University of Gothenburg.

Taleb, N.N. (2012), *Antifragile: Things that gain from disorder* (Penguin).

Chapter 4

Dimson, E., Marsh, P. and Staunton, M. (2014), *Credit Suisse Global Investment Returns Sourcebook 2014* (Credit Suisse AG).

Dimson, E. and Marsh, P. (2014), *Numis Smaller Companies Index Annual Review 2014* (Numis Securities).

Fama, E. and French, F. (1998), 'Value versus Growth: The International Evidence', *Journal of Finance*, 53 (6), 1975–1999.

Chapter 5

Arcot, S., Black, B. and Owen, G. (2007), 'From local to Global: The rise of AIM as a stock market for growing companies', London School of Economics and Political Science.

AIM: A Guide to AIM Tax Benefits, Baker Tilly/London Stock Exchange.

Dimson, E. and Marsh, P. (2014), *Numis Smaller Companies Index Annual Review 2014* (Numis Securities).

Ibbotson, R.G., Chen, Z., Kim, D.Y-J., Hu, W.Y. (2013), 'Liquidity as an Investment Style', *Financial Analysts Journal*, vol. 69, no. 3.

Harrington, J. (2013), 'A good year to take AIM', *Proactive Investors*, 2 January 2014.

Quinlan, J.P. (2014), 'The Smell of Money', US Trust, Bank of America Private Wealth Management.

Chapter 6

'The Distributional Effects of Asset Purchases', Bank of England, 12 July 2012.

'A Vision for Rebalancing the Economy: A new approach to growth', CBI, 30 December 2011.

'Taper tantrums', *Financial Times*, 16 August 2013.

Gordon, R.J. (2012), 'Is US economic growth over? Faltering innovation confronts the six headwinds', *Centre for Economic Policy Research* (Northwestern University and CEPR), *Policy Insight*, no. 63.

Haltiwanger, J.C., Jarmin, R.S. and Miranda, J. (2010), 'Who Creates Jobs? Small vs. Large vs. Young?', National Bureau of Economic Research, working paper 16300.

Hill, R.A. and Dunbar, R.I.M. (2003), 'Social Network Size in Humans', *Human Nature* (Walter de Gruyter), vol. 14, no. 1.

Hunt, A. (2014), 'The Threat of Deflation Returns – The New Battle for Price Stability', Andrew Hunt Economics.

'Abolishing stamp duty on AIM shares is a bold and decisive policy from government', London Stock Exchange, 21 March 2013.

Morning headlines, *MacroStrategy Partnership*, 20 August 2014.

Quinlan, J.P. (2014), 'The Smell of Money', US Trust, Bank of America Private Wealth Management.

Roach, R. (2007), 'Corporate Power in a Global Economy', teaching module at Global Development And Environment Institute, Tufts University.

Standard & Poor's Global Fixed Income Research (2014), 'Global Corporate Issuers Face $8.9 Trillion In Rated Debt Maturities Through Year-End 2018', 14 March 2014.

Key Facts about UK Financial and Related Professional Services, TheCityUK, 6 January 2014.

'Apple and Microsoft have bigger cash holdings than the UK', *Daily Telegraph*, 13 April 2014.

UK Office for Budgetary Responsibility (2014), 'Economic and Fiscal Outlook', March 2014.

Wright, P., Upward, R. and Hijzen, A. (2010), 'Job creation, job destruction and the role of small firms', Leverhulme Centre for Research on Globalisation and Economic Policy, *Oxford Bulletin of Economics & Statistics* (Blackwell).

Chapter 7

Arnott, R., Li, F. and Sherrerd, K. (2008), 'Clairvoyant Value and the Value Effect', Research Affiliates.

Barclays Stockbrokers, Fund Tools, Top Funds, UK Smaller Companies sector (as on 22 May 2014).

Dimson, E. and Marsh, P. (2014), *Numis Smaller Companies Index Annual Review 2014* (Numis Securities).

Dimson, E., Marsh, P. and Staunton, M. (2014), *Credit Suisse Global Investment Returns Sourcebook 2014* (Credit Suisse AG).

Economic Cycle Research Unit (2014), 'Cognitive Dissonance at the Fed?', 30 May 2014.

Evans, R. (2013), 'Birth of the IHT-free Isa as ban on Aim shares is lifted', *The Telegraph*, 1 July 2013.

Financial Analysts Journal interview with Benjamin Graham (1976): www.bylo.org/bgraham76.html

Graham, B. (1949). *The Intelligent Investor: The Definitive Book on Value Investing* (4th edition: Harper & Row).

Knox, R.E. and Inkster, J.A. (1968), 'Post-decision dissonance at post time', *Journal of Personality and Social Psychology*, 8, pp.319–323. Cited by Wilson, G. (2013), 'The Psychology of Money', lecture at Gresham College, London.

'A guide to listing on the London Stock Exchange', London Stock Exchange (2010).

Stanovitch, K.E., West, R.F. and Toplak, M.E. (2013), 'Myside bias, rational thinking, and intelligence', *Current Directions in Psychological Science*, vol. 22, no.4.

Williams, G. (2011), *Slow Finance* (Bloomsbury).

Chapter 8

'Junk Bonds at $2 Trillion as Gundlach Pulls Back: Credit Markets', *Bloomberg*, 19 March 2014.

Economic Cycle Research Unit (2014), 'Cognitive Dissonance at the Fed?', 30 May 2014.

'US share buybacks and dividends hit record', *Financial Times*, 18 June 2014.

Hunt, A. (2014), 'Can the FRB Afford to Tighten? Will it Do So Anyway?', *Weekly Global Review*, 4 July 2014.

Hunt, A. (2014), *Weekly Global Review*, 15 August 2014.

UK National Archives, IMF Crisis: **www.nationalarchives.gov.uk/cabinetpapers/ themes/imf-crisis.htm**

McKinsey & Company (2012), 'Debt and Deleveraging: Uneven progress on the path to growth', January 2012.

Index